Volume II
OBJECTIVE SETTING
AND THE MBO PROCESS

MANAGEMENT BY OBJECTIVES

A SELF-INSTRUCTIONAL APPROACH

MANAGEMENT BY OBJECTIVES

A SELF-INSTRUCTIONAL APPROACH

WILLIAM C. GIEGOLD
Virginia Polytechnic Institute and State University

Volume II

OBJECTIVE SETTING AND THE MBO PROCESS

McGRAW-HILL BOOK COMPANY

New York / St. Louis / San Francisco / Auckland / Bogotá / Düsseldorf
Johannesburg / London / Madrid / Mexico / Montreal / New Delhi / Panama
Paris / São Paulo / Singapore / Sydney / Tokyo / Toronto

Library of Congress Cataloging in Publication Data

Giegold, William C
　　Management by objectives.

　　CONTENTS:　v. 1.　Strategic planning and the MBO process. — v.　2.
Objective setting and the MBO process. — v.　3.　Per-
formance appraisal and the MBO process.
　　1.　Management by objectives — Collected works.
I.　Title.
HD30.12.G53　　　658.4　　　78–14764
ISBN 0-07-023191-5

OBJECTIVE SETTING AND THE MBO PROCESS
Volume II

MANAGEMENT BY OBJECTIVES: A Self-Instructional Approach

1234567890 DODO 78321098

This book was set in Univers by Allen Wayne Technical Corp.
The editors were Robert G. Manley and John Hendry;
the designer was Anne Canevari Green;
the production supervisor was Jeanne Selzam.
R. R. Donnelley & Sons Company was printer and binder.

CONTENTS

PREFACE

This is the second volume of a three-volume series entitled *Management by Objectives: A Self-Instructional Approach.* The series is intended to achieve the following objectives:

1. To facilitate one's understanding of the management system known as Management by Objectives, or MBO for short.

2. To identify and describe the elements which make up the MBO system and the interpersonal skills which enhance the chances of its successful implementation.

3. To give the reader an opportunity to develop the required skills and to experience some of the problems and pitfalls that may arise in implementing MBO.

4. To help the reader develop a management system which adapts the general principles of MBO to the specific needs of his or her organization.

Each volume may be used independently of the others by those readers or organizations whose needs lie predominantly in the areas covered by only one or two of the books. In this volume we cover the processes of setting objectives and formulating action plans, as described below. Volume I concentrates on the strategic planning process and Volume III deals with performance appraisal.

The three volumes are self-instructional since they allow an individual reader, by completing the exercises, to apply the principles of MBO to his or her own organization or job and thus have a first-hand knowledge of the problems and pitfalls one may encounter when introducing MBO into an organization. If you are a manager, completion of this self-study will give you the ability and confidence to install such a system in your own component, with little or no outside assistance. The *Leader's Manual* which accompanies the series gives further help to any reader who takes on the responsibility of conducting MBO training for others in an organization—employees or coworkers—in a group setting.

This volume, like each of the others in the series, begins with a general overview of the MBO system. It then turns to the objective-setting process. The setting of clear, challenging objectives is often regarded as the heart of the MBO process—the element that makes the difference between MBO and any other system of management. Anyone who has wrestled with the problems of teaching, introducing, or evaluating MBO would agree that objective setting is important enough for us to devote a separate volume to it.

Why was this not made the *first* volume in the series, but instead sandwiched in between the volumes devoted to strategic planning and performance appraisal? Partly because of the sequence in which these activities occur in practice.* But there is a more important reason. Many MBO failures result from overemphasis on the mechanics of setting objectives and a corresponding neglect of the planning and review functions.

In the early days of MBO, such an overemphasis led for a time to the position taken by many authorities that the key word in management by objectives is *management.* But Peter Drucker, in his latest series of management training films, gives the pendulum a forceful

---

*Figure 1 in the text highlights the steps of the overall process covered in this volume. This figure appears in Unit 1 of each of the three volumes in this series, and gives an explanation of each step.

push in the opposite direction, maintaining that the recent pre-occupation with management by managers has blinded them to the need for examining their objectives more closely.

Our main purpose in placing this volume on objective-setting techniques in the middle of the series is to put it in its proper place as an essential but totally interdependent part of the integrated process that MBO must be in order to live up to its potential. Whatever their importance in the scheme of things, carelessly or arbitrarily set objectives are a major source of the problems associated with MBO. This volume is designed to help you avoid or at least minimize such problems.

For example, a frustrating experience frequently encountered in the early phases of MBO is the repeated slippage of projected dates for accomplishment. This often results in the eventual discrediting of the whole process by managers who have pinned their hopes on "challenging" objectives to provide the impetus for improved performance. We will prescribe remedies for this condition in the form of validation techniques designed to increase the probability of successful achievement.

For an objective to be valid, the plan for its accomplishment must be recognized as an intrinsic part of the objective itself. This volume treats the process of action planning as an integral part of objective setting.

In a sense, objective writing and action planning are the parts of the MBO process that are easiest to grasp because they closely resemble methods and practices already used by most effective and successful organizations. Although this may seem familiar ground to readers who are members of such organizations, we urge you to cover it carefully, because a superficial understanding of the objective-setting process is a source of many pitfalls.

Throughout this volume and the next we will be speaking of the "manager" or "boss" and the "subordinate" or the "employee" in dealing with the person-to-person interaction that forms the heart of objective setting and review under an MBO system. Depending on his or her position in the organization, the employee may also be a manager either of individuals or of other managers. Hired managers (even the chief executive officer) in any organization will find themselves acting in both roles if MBO is implemented properly—from the top down. Therefore, as you read and as you complete the exercises, try to place yourself in the role of employee as well as in that of boss.

This will not only familiarize you with both roles, but also help you develop the empathy that is so important to the interaction required by an effectively functioning MBO system.

––––––––––

No book in a field as broad as management is the work of the writer alone. We acknowledge the immense contributions of forerunners whose works are cited herein, as well as many unnamed others whose thoughts provided the springboard for this work. A special debt of gratitude is due to Mike Crump of Syracuse University's School of Management, who conceived the idea for this series but who unfortunately was unable to play his rightful role in making it come to pass.

We thank Frank Mahoney, Art Kirn, and C. C. Schmidt for their painstaking reviews of the manuscript and their helpful suggestions, many of which they will find incorporated within. Project manager John Hendry has shown great patience and skill in keeping the author's feet on the ground. He and the McGraw-Hill staff—Bob Manley, Bob Leap, Anne Green, and the many copy editors, artists, compositors, and others who have put a bit of themselves into these books—would command any author's admiration and respect.

Finally, to Irma, who typed the manuscripts and whose editing of the raw material made the job much easier for the professionals, goes more than thanks for her loving support throughout.

William C. Giegold

Volume II
OBJECTIVE SETTING
AND THE MBO PROCESS

MANAGEMENT BY OBJECTIVES
A SELF-INSTRUCTIONAL APPROACH

UNIT 1

INTRODUCTION

AN OVERVIEW OF THE MANAGEMENT BY OBJECTIVES SYSTEM

The phrase "management by objectives," or MBO for short, has become a part of the language of management throughout the world. Managers, supervisors, and others in responsible positions at every level in almost every type and size of organization, from churches to the military, and from the multinational corporation to the family-owned hardware store, are on speaking acquaintance with the concept. It has appeared under several names — results-oriented management, management by objectives and results (MBO/R), work planning and review, "planagement," and management by agreement, to list a few. The names reveal the particular emphasis or bias of their authors. One stresses the planning aspects. Another emphasizes the give-and-take by which bosses and subordinates agree on their mutual goals. Others reflect merely their authors' dissatisfaction with the ability of the original name — MBO — to convey the full meaning and purpose of the management system to which it refers.

Whatever its title, the principles of this system remain the same, as valid as they were when originally proposed a quarter of a century ago. They compose the most rational system of "total management" yet developed. In spite of this, unfortunately, the potential of the system remains today largely as promise rather than realization. The ranks of those who have "tried it" in a superficial or halfhearted way and been disappointed far outnumber those who have understood it and had the will to submit to its demands. Those who have done so can testify to its merits. They can also testify to the fact that it is a *demanding* system of management.

In this guided tour of the system we will stop frequently and let you experience for yourself the extent of the commitment you must make to excellence in the profession of management when you opt for MBO. Whether you are the top person in your organization, a first-line manager, or not yet appointed to your first management job — and whether or not your organization formally adopts an MBO system — you can become a much more effective manager by putting to work on the job what you practice in this series of books.

A DEFINITION OF MANAGEMENT BY OBJECTIVES

"Management by objectives" has been defined by George Odiorne as:

> " . . .a *management* process *whereby the supervisor and the subordinate, operating under a* clear definition of *the common* goals *and* priorities *of the organization established by* top management, jointly *identify the individual's major* areas of responsibility *in terms of the* results expected *of him or her, and* use *these* measures *as guides for operating the unit and assessing the* contributions *of each of its members.*[1] "

Written in the early days of MBO, this definition has retained its currency and covers very concisely the essential features of this system of management. It is rich in meanings which do not reveal them-

---

[1]George S. Odiorne, *Management by Objectives: A System of Managerial Leadership* (New York: Pitman, 1965), pp. 55-56.

selves until it has been examined word for word. We have emphasized several key words and phrases, and will point out their significance below. In this volume and the others in this series, we will expand on each of these points to provide a thorough knowledge of the principles of MBO and how to put them to work in your organization. We will also relate them to your effectiveness as an individual, on and off the job.

The key words are these:

process—MBO, like management itself, is a continuing activity, not a "campaign," a "program," or a onetime installation project which when completed can produce results on its own. It is an endless cyclical group of interrelated management activities embodying all the conventional management functions of planning, organizing, directing, and controlling. We show it as a flowchart in Fig. 1, and will explain the steps later in this unit.

clear definition of goals—This is the thrust which the name MBO implies. Clearly defined goals or objectives provide the focus of effort which is required for the most efficient use of resources. ("Goal" and "objective" are interchangeable terms. We will primarily use the latter throughout this series.)

priorities—Objectives are not enough to ensure organizational or individual effectiveness. One must be sure that the most important objectives are tackled first, and a system for establishing priorities is a vital link in the overall process.

top management—If the clear definition of goals and priorities begins at the very top, the system achieves it fullest potential, since all parts of the organization set their sights on the same overall target. Top management also plays a continuing role in emphasizing the need for organizational improvement. The single strongest motivating factor in a successful MBO system is top management's support of and demand for the degree of management effort required by MBO.

jointly—In the MBO effort, the process of joint objective setting by the manager and the employee is the key to obtaining full cooperation and acceptance by employees. This same process is also the means by which the full knowledge and creative potential of the employee are brought to bear on the improvement needs of the organization.

areas of responsibility—Every position or job must exist for a purpose well defined in relationship to the needs of the organization. This relationship is established through the *key results areas* (KRAs) of the organization, which determine the job responsibilities most important to overall needs, and guide the search for meaningful objectives. (We will have more to say about key results areas in due course.)

results expected—The apparent emphasis on objectives in MBO may seem to neglect the purpose for which the whole effort is designed: *to produce results which would not otherwise be achieved.* Stating the expectations of management is a most potent way of communicating with employees. Expressing these expectations in terms of the needed results replaces vague exhortations or, worse yet, the silence which communicates management's acceptance of the status quo.

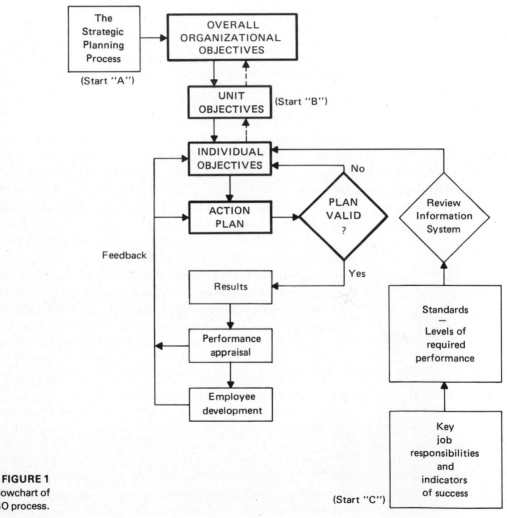

FIGURE 1
A flowchart of
the MBO process.

use ("to use," an *active* verb) — The establishment of objectives at all levels in an organization is an important part of the MBO system, but in too many cases it has been mistaken for the *purpose* of the system. A campaign is mounted, individuals and managers at all levels strain mightily to produce volume upon volume of objectives — and the results are placed on the shelf, to be removed only to demonstrate proudly that "we have MBO."

measures — Unless the objectives are *used* to measure progress and the measurements are then used to make adjustments and corrections which *accelerate* progress, MBO remains static and sterile, rather than becoming the dynamic and productive system it is designed to be.

contributions — MBO encourages the contributions of every individual to the overall objectives of the organization, measures each contribution, and provides the basis for rewards in proportion.

THE PURPOSE OF MBO: IMPROVED EFFECTIVE- NESS

A key word left out of Odiorne's description, and the primary reason for considering MBO for your organization, is "improvement." What we are working on here is improvement in both organizational and individual effectiveness. The most productive way to look at an objective is as an *improvement need* relative to the situation as it is now or as it is forecast to become unless deliberate action is taken. We stress this word and this concept of an objective because of the tendency to set objectives which merely document what the organization is already doing. Such an approach may satisfy all the formalities, but it turns MBO into a ritual rather than a thrust toward improvement.

A second reason for considering MBO, as we have suggested, is that it provides guidance in the conduct of the management process itself. As a framework for organizing managerial thought and activity, MBO satisfies all the needs of a manager who is attempting to follow the prescriptions of management authorities such as Peter Drucker. Drucker's concept of the management job requires first answering the question: "What are the purposes and nature of our organization, and what *should* they be?" Next, clear objectives and goals are established, with priorities and measures of performance. Then a climate is created in which employees exercise self-correction and self-control by maintaining a continuing audit of the results and the objectives themselves, and adjusting their efforts as needed.

The correspondence between Odiorne's definition of MBO and Drucker's summary of the total management job is striking. It identifies MBO as a *system of management* rather than, in the view often taken, as a management tool or technique to be superimposed on "everything else that we are already doing."

THE MBO SYSTEM: A BRIEF DESCRIPTION   Figure 1 illustrates the system in flowchart form. The highlighted portions, objective setting and action planning, are covered in this second volume of the three-volume series. Volume I deals with individual and organizational strategic planning; Vol. III is devoted to performance appraisal.

Here, step by step, is how the whole thing works:

The strategic planning activity   MBO does not "start with objectives," but with strategic planning. (See starting point A in Fig. 1.) This process is necessary to determine what kinds of objectives are compatible with the purposes, strengths, and resources of the organization. Before attempting to set organizational objectives, strategic planning answers two major questions: "Why are we here?" and "Who are we?" Only after these questions have been answered can we intelligently ask the third question: "Where are we going?" Answering the first two questions involves self-analysis by the organization, competitive and environmental analysis, and a series of comparisons — with *competitors'* achievements and with *our own potential* — to determine organizational strengths and weaknesses. This analysis, initiated by top management, determines how resources can best be concentrated and deployed, a maneuver we call "strategy selection."

Although strategic planning is initiated by top management for the organization as a whole, the type of thinking it entails is equally important for a smaller component of the organization, and even for the individual employee or manager. In the first volume of this series, we discuss at length how these principles can be applied to a person's job or career strategy.

Overall organizational objectives These are the short-range and long-range targets for organizational improvement established by the highest level of management. They are the basis for much of the objective setting done at lower levels in the organization, as each unit or component determines its contribution to the overall objective.

Overall organizational objectives, like all objectives in the MBO system, have three main purposes. These are to:

1. Function as records of commitments made by their authors
2. Serve as a yardstick for measuring progress
3. Act as positive motivators of achievement

To be fully functional, an objective must be prepared with a number of stringent requirements continually in mind. Some of the more obvious are clarity, specificity, measurability, and, surprisingly perhaps, achievability. High-sounding, ambitious objectives that exceed their author's capability, resources, or authority weaken an MBO system by destroying its credibility. We will cover the detailed requirements of sound objectives in Unit 3.

Unit objectives All units are called on to contribute to the organization's objectives, as noted above. This does not mean, however, that the component must wait to be directed, nor does it mean that the component cannot initiate objectives based on the firsthand view of the situation which only its members enjoy. The reverse (dashed) arrows in Fig. 1 signify the unit's influence on the overall organizational objectives and its responsibility to feed its firsthand knowledge into the system.

While the strategic planning process is the ideal starting point (A on the flowchart) for an organization adopting an MBO system, a single unit may be used as the starting point for a pilot effort (point B). If this alternative is taken, there is still a need to assure conformance with overall organizational needs, and to think strategically about the resource deployment of the unit before deciding on its objectives.

Individual objectives On the flowchart (Fig. 1) individual objectives are the focal point for much of the flow of information and action in the MBO process. The individual is the ultimate contributor to overall organizational objectives as well as to unit objectives. Note that, as the reverse arrow indicates, the individual also has the opportunity and the responsibility to shape and modify the higher-level objectives. Later in this unit we will describe the other flows which terminate in this block of the diagram.

Figure 2 illustrates how the individual responds to an overall need for profit improvement in a multilevel organization. As the overall targets are considered at successively lower levels, the resulting objectives will normally become much more detailed and narrower in scope.

Note that the arrows depicting the flow of the objective-setting process point in both directions. This indicates the dynamic nature of the process, in which the ideas responding to the overall need flow *up,* while the motivating force for the generation of the nature and size of the total contributions needed flows *down.* The upward flow also implies that the total of manufacturing and other functional contributions must be examined closely against the overall need in order to determine the adequacy of the overall cost reduction effort. For example, if all individual and subfunctional manufacturing contributions only add up to $450,000 of cost reduction available in 19___ from manufacturing, the manufacturing objective itself must be reexamined.

It is also possible, however, that the corporate profit improvement target was set without enough thought to its achievability, or that it relies too heavily on cost reduction rather than on sales volume, pricing, and other contributors to profit improvement. The setting of overall organizational objectives is discussed with the strategic planning process in Vol. I.

Plan for action   As we will explain in Unit 3 of this volume, the detailed plan for reaching an objective is an essential part of the objective itself. It details who is going to do what, when, and with whose help. The plan fulfills three important functions: it describes how the objective will be reached and therefore enhances the validity and credibility of the objective, it budgets the time and other resources required of those responsible, and it is used for monitoring progress toward the ultimate objective.

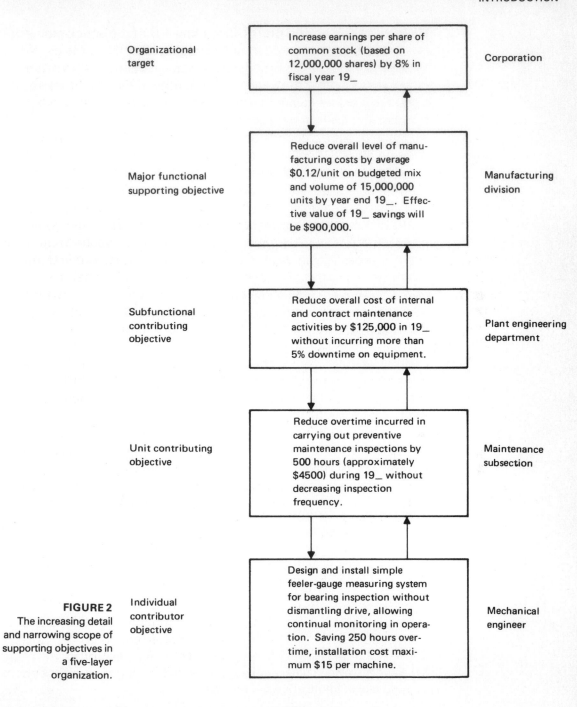

| Organizational target | Increase earnings per share of common stock (based on 12,000,000 shares) by 8% in fiscal year 19_ | Corporation |

| Major functional supporting objective | Reduce overall level of manufacturing costs by average $0.12/unit on budgeted mix and volume of 15,000,000 units by year end 19_. Effective value of 19_ savings will be $900,000. | Manufacturing division |

| Subfunctional contributing objective | Reduce overall cost of internal and contract maintenance activities by $125,000 in 19_ without incurring more than 5% downtime on equipment. | Plant engineering department |

| Unit contributing objective | Reduce overtime incurred in carrying out preventive maintenance inspections by 500 hours (approximately $4500) during 19_ without decreasing inspection frequency. | Maintenance subsection |

| Individual contributor objective | Design and install simple feeler-gauge measuring system for bearing inspection without dismantling drive, allowing continual monitoring in operation. Saving 250 hours overtime, installation cost maximum $15 per machine. | Mechanical engineer |

FIGURE 2
The increasing detail and narrowing scope of supporting objectives in a five-layer organization.

Validity of the action plan Close scrutiny of the action plan itself is one of the best methods for validating an objective — that is, for assuring that it has a high probability of achievement. Such scrutiny determines whether the quality and quantity of the resources assigned to it are adequate. It also serves as a check on the quality of the planning itself. Any major flaws revealed at this point will require a change of plan, a change of objective, or both, as indicated by the decision branch ("no" or "yes") in the flowchart.

There are other opportunities to validate an action plan. One is the joint objective-setting discussion mentioned in Odiorne's definition. This procedure assures that the manager and the employee are jointly committed to achieving the objective. The manager commits his or her effort in helping the employee surmount obstacles and attain success. To arrive at that agreement, the manager first must be convinced of the desirability and validity of the employee's proposed objective. Two heads thus applied to the examination of the proposed objective make more than doubly certain that its conception is sound.

Results This small single block on the flowchart represents the reason your organization exists — the production of goods or services. Lest we appear to be slighting this most important concern of every organization, we remind you that the primary purpose of everything else we are discussing is the *continual improvement of results* through better planning, direction, and feedback.

Performance review Each employee should continually review and appraise results, and this self-review and appraisal should be supplemented by periodic formal discussions between manager and employee. These activities breathe life into what otherwise might become a static and nonproductive exercise in planning. The review process consists of:

1. The day-by-day assessment of progress
2. The continual problem solving which keeps things moving
3. Periodic reviews wherein the manager and the employee assess results and replan future efforts, if necessary
4. The manager's infrequent but regular appraisal of the employee's performance and potential

The first three items are mainly concerned with the progress of the work itself, whereas the fourth is primarily employee-oriented. The first two, concerned with the day-to-day control of the work, are left in the hands of the employee, with help from the manager as needed. The periodic review and the performance appraisal, quarterly and annual respectively, are joint discussions with the manager. Performance review procedures are explained in detail in Vol. III.

Feedback   The results of the performance review and appraisal process are fed back into the ongoing objective-setting and action-planning process, and help determine changes in objectives and plans. Revision of individuals' objectives affect unit objectives as well. Feedback from the employee to the manager during the periodic review discussion may show that the employee needs the manager's help to clear obstacles from the path of progress. (Such efforts often become a part of the manager's personal objectives.) Feedback thus keeps the MBO system responsive to problems, deviations, and the need for corrective effort. The feedback does not stop at the level of the individual and the manager. Inputs from the individual level are often helpful to the strategic planning process and the reshaping of overall organizational objectives.

In the MBO process, "feedback" also means the information given to the employee about performance, in both the technical and the human relations aspects of the job. Much of this kind of feedback comes from the manager. For the employee, it fills very important psychological needs for recognition and for knowing "how I'm doing" in the eyes of the boss. It is also important that the employee have access to feedback in the form of reports or other measurement tools that give *direct* information about progress without the intervention of the manager. This kind of feedback allows the employee to exert a maximum of self-control and responsibility on the job.

Employee development   The performance review may indicate that the employee needs further training or other forms of development in order to perform the present job effectively or to prepare for future positions that may be suggested by the performance-and-potential appraisal. The MBO system may become a highly mechanistic form of management unless managers maintain and demonstrate a genuine interest in their employees' personal and professional development. This is essential to the realization of the full benefits the system offers.

We will discuss the potential benefits of both the mechanistic and the employee-centered application of MBO later in this unit, but first the series of processes leading to the individual objectives step in the Fig. 1 flowchart must be explained. These processes are essential prerequisites to the individual objective-setting process. In effect, they represent strategic planning at the "micro" level, focusing on the individual. They are analogous in many respects to the "macro" process of strategy formulation for the organization as a whole.

Individual responsibilities Each jobholder must have a clear understanding of the reasons for the existence of the job, its key responsibilities, and the priorities each of these responsibilities carries. This may seem a truism, but it is often overlooked. The well-known example of customer service specialists who regard phone calls from customers as interruptions which prevent them from catching up on paperwork illustrates the need to get back to basics — on the part of the manager as well as the specialist!

Lacking (or losing) this perspective on the important contributions the job must provide, the employee may become embroiled in time-consuming activity that contributes little to the desired results. The employee's efforts will tend to become increasingly misdirected unless the relationship between the job and the organizational mission is kept in mind. To avoid this problem, a thorough understanding of the key results areas of the organization is essential. The KRAs are those aspects of total performance in which an organization must continually set and achieve objectives for improvement to preserve its health and assure its growth.

It is also important for every employee to have a model of mature, expert performance — or, more specifically, an indicator of success for each important responsibility, answering the question "How will I know when this part of my job is being done well?" These indicators should be incorporated in the job description or other document defining the job.

Job descriptions are not a new concept. All organizations use them to list the duties of the jobholder, to give information to prospective candidates for the job, and as a guide to selection of the right individual in terms of abilities, experience, and interests. In some cases, the employee may pull his or her own job description out of the files from time to time, and refer to it as a checklist to see whether all the bases are being covered. Managers may refer to the job descriptions of their subordinates at appraisal time to refresh their memories on exactly what each person is supposed to be doing. However, the MBO process requires more than a mere list of the duties which a jobholder is expected to perform from time to time while occupying the position. The inputs from the lower right portion of Fig. 1 (leading to the individual's objectives), which provide the link between the unit or component objectives and what the individual actually contributes, come from a more sophisticated version of the job description than a mere listing of duties.

The position guide, or job description, in the MBO system specifies levels of performance for each duty or responsibility. It indicates the achievement level which a fully trained and mature incumbent would be expected to reach on the job — the ultimate in performance. Obviously, not every incumbent, especially in the first months or even years on the job, can reasonably be expected to achieve these ultimate levels of performance — certainly not if jobs are designed to provide opportunities for growth. Interim levels which *can* be achieved are therefore established to provide shorter-range targets for the new incumbent, since the "impossible dream" may not be the most appropriate motivator for the newcomer. We will describe the content and uses of an MBO job description in Unit 3.

You may question the value of having two sets of targets for the individual. An analogy may be found in long-distance running. For many years, long-distance runners held the 4-minute mile as an "unachievable" but prized goal. Before that elusive record was reached, there were of course many winners along the way. Performances of long-distance runners became steadily more impressive in part because that goal existed. Along the way, however, it is probable that most runners found their real motivation in an attempt to better the fastest previous performance or to knock another second off their own best previous time.

Levels of performance Establishing levels of performance in the form of standards of excellence — the highest achievements in the field — helps keep in view the opportunities for improvement in the routine, continuing duties of any job. In the rare case, present performance may be at such a masterful level already. Here the standard can act as a baseline for measuring deterioration in performance if it occurs. In any case, the objectives of each individual must be apportioned between the routine and the often more interesting and appealing creative projects. Having a level of ultimate performance as a reminder encourages attention to the routine.

The information system   Measurements of performance are readily established and verified in some cases, but not in others. The expense of time and effort in gathering the data necessary to assess performance against a measurement criterion that was hastily proposed can be great. The capabilities of the existing information system must be examined carefully when you prepare standards. Often information presently available will suggest a form in which the standards can be expressed without generating new data.

In any case, the climate of self-control mentioned earlier requires that the information be made available directly to the employee in a timely fashion. Ideally, the employee is the *first to become aware* of problems and has the maximum opportunity to correct them.

A STARTING POINT FOR INDIVIDUAL- IZED MBO   When this chain of prerequisite planning processes has been completed, the individual is in a position to select most effectively the objectives pertinent to the job. Once these processes are completed to the mutual satisfaction of manager and employee, the output, usually in the form of a job description of the type described above, should become a *working tool* for both, not merely a part of the permanent organization manual for the unit (which normally just gathers dust in someone's file drawer or bookcase). At the very least it should be used to prepare for the periodic performance appraisal and to guide newcomers on the job.

Preparation of such a detailed job description constitutes a method whereby you, the individual employee or manager, can institute your own test of MBO. We have designated starting point C on the flowchart as the point of entry for the individual. Though it is possible to carry out some of the essential parts of the process by yourself, the review of your performance will of course be much less subjective if you enlist the help of your immediate manager. Doing so will also give a broader perspective on organizational KRAs, unit objectives, and other inputs you will need. (It is not necessary to have formal companywide KRAs or objectives in effect. You can generate a reasonable facsimile — enough to serve this limited purpose — in dialogue with your manager.) If you are a manager, you may wish to try this same approach by selecting an employee to conduct the test of the system. If you decide to do this, don't overlook your own responsibilities in making the system work. We have referred to these responsibilities earlier, and will discuss them at length in Unit 8.

WHAT CAN THE ORGANIZATION EXPECT OF MBO?

MBO holds promise for an organization in proportion to the difference between its management system and the one we have described — not as its system appears on paper, but as it actually operates, and *whether or not* it is referred to as "management by objectives." There are exceptions to this rule of thumb. A military or other organization that has operated traditionally with strong direction from the top may actually be thrown off stride — at least temporarily — by the introduction of concepts such as joint objective setting and self-control. All organizations have members who thrive under strongly directive leadership. These individuals may not respond immediately to the humanistic — that is, employee-centered — aspects of MBO.

At the other end of the scale, an organization may be composed of highly creative self-starters, whose output is "discovery" and whose mode is to follow the lead suggested by the most recent experiment in designing the next one. Such people are likely to be turned off by the order, structure, and "mechanization" they see in the MBO approach.

In each of these polar extremes, however, there are potential company benefits from the judicious introduction of the humanistic elements in the first case and the mechanistic or structural improvements in the second. For most organizations the benefits of the MBO system come eventually from both sources. In fact, a management system cannot properly be called MBO unless it does involve both humanistic and structural elements.

The structural elements foster the sense of common direction, the clarity of purpose, the focus on results and standards, and the level of communication and management feedback which the audit and control functions of MBO provide. More specifically, the ultimate benefit derives from:

Effectiveness rather than mere efficiency, "doing the right things" in addition to "doing things right"

More efficient and purposeful communication between levels of management and between employees and their managers

An improved mechanism for rational planning, emphasizing strengths while recognizing weaknesses, the competitive environment, and the needs of the organization's clients or "claimants"

A more rational method for evaluating and rewarding the contributors to success, based on performance rather than on personality traits

A generally more cohesive and informed work force, in which individuals concentrate their efforts on common goals and priorities

The humanistic elements of MBO foster employee autonomy and self-control, participation in the decision-making process, and the feedback which is clearly concerned with the individual's personal development. These are central themes of the mutual objective setting and the performance appraisal and review processes. The benefits appear in the form of a better-performing work force resulting from:

Employees' higher degree of commitment to activities, decisions, and programs which they have played a significant part in creating

Their greater trust of and cooperation with managers because of the helping attitude the latter exhibit toward them

Their realization that rewards depend not only on what gets done, but on how it is accomplished — recognizing the employees' problem-solving and coping behavior, and in general treating them as unique individuals

The interest shown in their personal growth and development

The *immediate* potential for your organization may lie in either one or both of these areas. The organization which is in disarray may well concentrate its effort first on restructuring, and may institute the humanistic emphasis at a later point. We note such an evolution especially in the performance appraisal system. The pre-MBO system is more than likely a checklist of personality traits (cooperativeness, attitude, initiative, etc.). The structural emphasis of MBO puts appraisal on much firmer ground: performance. The humanistic emphasis puts back into the equation a personality dimension, as noted above, but one which must not overlook the measures of objective performance.

To summarize, taking a polar position on the "true" meaning and purpose of MBO can result in failure to utilize its full potential. An organization may profitably introduce the system in either way, mechanistic or humanistic, depending on the present status of its management system — but always with an eye to the future benefits of going all the way.

WHAT MBO IS NOT: SOME MISCONCEP- TIONS

Through the years a number of misconceptions have arisen to be-cloud the MBO issue. They point up the widespread superficiality of understanding to which we referred earlier. Aggravated by over-enthusiastic claims by MBO's promoters, and by the horror stories related by those who attempted to apply it without sufficient preparation, these misconceptions have created a negative climate in many organizations, preventing a rational discussion of MBO as a potential improvement in management practice. We conclude this brief overview of MBO with a list of prevalent claims and statements to which we add a few words of refutation or clarification.

"Another new gimmick, soon forgotten . . ."

By now we hope you understand that MBO is not a gimmick, but rather a system of total management. Furthermore, it is not new. It is an articulation of management functions and processes that characterize the work of the better managers in the most effective organizations. First defined and described in the 1950s, it is not likely to die out or be forgotten as long as there is a need for creative managers dedicated to organizational improvement.

"A highly complex and theoretical concept developed in the ivory tower by academicians"

True, the concepts were first articulated in the universities, but by management authorities with a decidedly real-world orientation.

These researchers and consultants made a real contribution by documenting and systematizing the very practical methods developed by their clients.

"Purports to be an 'easy out' for managers . . ."

This could not be further from the truth. MBO is a most demanding system of management. There is, as far as we know, no easy road to effective management over the long term. Some proponents have described the system as simply an informal, periodic, verbal, or "back of an envelope" contract between a manager and an employee, promising vast results. The contract is indeed a part of MBO, but the results depend on a great deal more than that.

"A panacea for all organizational ills . . ."

Insofar as good management practices can identify and ultimately solve many problems in the organization, MBO can qualify as a "broad-spectrum" antidote. But it is no cure for incompetence, and no insurance against such forces as inflation, foreign competition, and government intervention. Its practice will build competence, but it also *requires* competence. And it can help the organization adapt to, if not foresee and avoid, the impact of the uncontrollable factors.

"A typical 'campaign': a big flurry and it's all over . . ."

Unfortunately, this is the form the implementation takes in many organizations. The initial effort is to produce a set of objectives. All levels of management set to work, the big book is published, and the whole organization lapses into a state of normalcy until the next campaign. But such an approach, as we have seen, does not produce an MBO system.

"Only for large production organizations, where output can be 'counted'"

Operations whose output can be counted tend to have an easier time of setting objectives, but they benefit most from the objectives they set in the intangible areas. Organizations large or small, whose output is all intangible—a school guidance office, for instance—need MBO even more than the production operation.

"A 'paper mill' that bogs you down in a morass of forms and reports . . ."

This is probably the most legitimate of all the critical comments on our list. Documentation *can* become a major problem. However, it can be kept under control. We will have some suggestions on avoiding the hazards of paperwork in Units 4 and 6.

"A punitive approach to managing people . . ."

This belief comes from early attempts to simplify performance appraisal by measuring only how fully an employee met the stated objectives. Since the employee was supposed to set the objective in the first place, MBO quickly got the reputation of "giving them enough rope to hang themselves." Needless to say, this feeling on the part of employees was something more than paranoia. This is

One common misconception is that MBO is a punitive approach to management. (Drawing by Whitney Darrow, Jr.; © 1977 The New Yorker Magazine, Inc.)

"Faster!"

still one of the most frequently encountered stumbling blocks in the way of implementing MBO. If these kinds of employee attitudes have been instilled by past management practices, managers must be very sensitive in handling the joint objective-setting process and in performance appraisal. At best it will take time and patience, through several cycles of appraisal and feedback, to get the point across that managers are there to help the employee be successful.

The other units of this volume deal with the processes of objective setting and action planning. Before turning to the next unit, however, work through the exercises for this unit. The first exercise will give you an opportunity to assess your job and your organization, as they are and as they might be affected by an MBO system of the type we have described. The second is a test of your understanding of the process.

Most of the units in this entire series are followed by one or more exercises. Try to complete each unit's exercises before reading on. You will get much more insight into the MBO process if you do so.

We will offer a few words of comment or interpretation following each exercise. This is to give you feedback on your performance wherever possible. In relatively few instances do we provide answers, because the proportion of cases or problems where anyone other than you can *know* the answer is small. Most exercises (like the two in this unit) involve analysis of your own job situation or organization, or they present situations into which *you* must project *yourself.* Our commentary, therefore, is often in the form of suggestions — about facets of the problem which are typically overlooked, or about further work you can do on your own to apply the principles and methods of MBO on the job.

You will find the exercises demanding of your thought, time, and energy. Do them thoughtfully and carefully. You will get much more out of the books if you complete *every* exercise, because the exercises address important points not covered in the text. You will better understand many of the difficulties that can arise in applying MBO principles by *first* exposing yourself to the problems in the exercises and *then* reading about their possible solutions.

Finally, remember what we said in the beginning, that MBO requires a great deal of commitment. How you respond to these exercises is a test of your commitment, and probably a good predictor of your success in tackling MBO.

EXERCISE 1A   1.   List the critically important duties, responsibilities, and results which your job should, under ideal conditions, contribute to the organization.

2.   List any other duties which interfere with your fulfilling the critical obligations listed above.

3. List any problems (organizational, procedural, policy, interpersonal, etc.) which prevent you from contributing to the organization as effectively as you wish.

4. Select the most critical interferences and problems you have identified. Referring to the MBO definition and flow process diagram (Fig. 1), in which aspect or element of MBO might you expect to find an answer or solution? Describe the possible actions you might take and the results you might expect from them.

EXERCISE 1B   We haven't truly learned a concept until we can explain it to others. Listed below are several questions which have come up in introductory seminars, from managers hearing about MBO for the first time. Test your understanding of the overall process as we have presented it in Unit 1 by responding to these neophytes. Fill in the key points of your response on the outline. Practice giving the full response verbally to an associate or to a mirror.

1.   "Why this laborious process of looking at major responsibilities or KRAs, thinking up 'ultimate levels of performance,' and *then* setting objectives? I know what my job is; it's to cut costs. Why not just let me set objectives — period?"

2.   "It sounds like MBO just consists of writing down what I'm already doing. This is only taking my time away from doing it, and then holding my feet to the fire because I don't bat a thousand."

3.   "A formal performance appraisal will do nothing but inflame my people! We don't have a merit pay system in our city. How can I motivate a person by giving her an excellent review and then not reward her with extra pay?"

4.   "Suppose my manager asks my unit to contribute a share of our division's overall cost reduction target. Wouldn't I be a fool to commit myself to a figure unless I already had action plans to tell me how I'd reach that figure?"

5.   "How can I be sure an employee isn't 'snowing' me with an easy objective by claiming that's all he can possibly do?"

6.   "This idea of 'joint' objective setting is ridiculous. My boss passes some of them down to me from on high and I propose some of my own to him. What's 'joint' about that? Doesn't it just mean that I accept his, and then whatever time is left I use to work on my own?"

Statement	Key Points in Response
1.	
2.	
3.	
4.	
5.	
6.	

Commentary on Exercise 1A   We suggest that you first review your entries in questions 1, 2, and 3 for clarity and specificity. If, for example, in part 3 you have tended to use one- or two-word entries such as "communication," "restrictive policy," "uncooperative coworkers," go back and give it more thought. Identifying workable solutions is difficult if the problem is not well defined. Once the problem areas are defined, however, you should find answers to many of them in the MBO process.

You may also have been tempted to look for solutions in the MBO system that are not there. MBO is not the answer to all the problems an organization can accumulate. It will not create competent managers or technicians out of incompetent ones (though it will help identify the areas where competence is lacking). Neither will it take you out of a business you should not be in (though it may force you to answer the question of why you are in it). Keep your expectations at a reasonable level and apply MBO to systemic problems of planning, communication, control, and growth. Over time it will even help eliminate basic problems that may appear to be insoluble.

This exercise and others that focus on your own situation lend themselves to group thinking and consensus seeking as well as to individual study. The *Leader's Manual* which accompanies the series is intended to help you work with others in group sessions designed to introduce an MBO system into your organization.

Commentary on Exercise 1B   Your replies to these questions might have included the following points:

1.   The simple answer is that knowing where you're going helps in taking the first step. However, concentrating on the short-range objective entails two additional risks. First, by jumping too quickly to a short-term objective you may be foreclosing the opportunity to do what the authorities on creativity call "divergent thinking," that is, thinking about a problem area (or key results area) broadly and thereby keeping your options open. Converging too quickly on a specific solution tends to close the gate on other, possibly better ideas, keeping them locked up in your subconscious. It also puts you in the position of coming up with a solution before you fully understand the problem. In this case, the problem which your organization is facing may require a greater contribution from you in an area other than cost — for example, in quality or customer service. Covering all the KRAs helps ensure that

your cost-oriented efforts won't hurt results in quality, safety, labor relations, or some other KRA perhaps even more important. (What *are* your KRAs?)

2. If objectives are truly just a statement of what you are already doing, you have missed the whole *objective* of managing by objectives — namely the improvement of individual and organizational effectiveness. Let's rethink your objectives. Start with KRAs and look at long-range goals. What is your job going to require of you in 5 or 10 years? You'd better start planning to get there *now*.

   If you feel that your boss is out to trap you, then your problem is more serious than your doubts about MBO — it's a problem of mistrust, and you should try to get to the bottom of it, whether or not you are operating in an MBO system.

3. Of course, you know your people better than anyone else — or do you? People *do* stay on their jobs for reasons other than pay. If your pay plan is being administered equitably, and if jobs are classified and priced so that your people can understand the structure, they should be able to accept the facts of life. (Have you *communicated* the pay plan to them?) Anyhow, it's a mistake to think that the appraisal itself is the motivator. The *real* motivation came from the opportunity to do that superior piece of work and from the achievement itself. A good performance review is merely good, positive recognition, which can help keep that motivation alive. It also affirms your interest in your employee's future growth. This interest may help *keep the employee around,* so that you'll have a good candidate when the next opportunity for a promotion or an upgrade comes along. Failure to give positive recognition to your better performers either risks losing them from the organization entirely or encourages them to perform at the lowest common denominator. With really good employees, it's usually the former that happens.

4. This is a "chicken or egg" question. Which comes first, the objective or the plan of action? In fact, the two are inseparable, and you really can't say that you have firmly established an objective until you have examined the courses of action open to you for achieving it. The process is one of matching needs and potential contributions, and there is no guarantee that the match will be perfect the first time around. It's somewhat easier to do when you are the initiator yourself and have an innovative proposal to reduce cost, for example. In this case your cost objective becomes your own evaluation of what the results of your efforts will be. But when responding to a higher level need, it's best to give an honest estimate of what your contribution will be. If a gap exists, set an objective of identifying ways to close it.

5. At the functional level in an organization, there is no substitute for a manager's knowledge of the workers and of the technology involved in the function for which the manager is responsible. If you are new to the organization, you will of course have to rely more heavily on your technical knowledge at first. The question, however, seems to overlook the fact that MBO requires a continually dynamic management style in which manager and subordinate continue to learn about each other. The observant, energetic manager will soon spot the performer whose tendency is to hold back. MBO cannot substitute for intelligence and effort on the part of managers.

6. Some organizational needs are nonnegotiable "musts." (The corporate profit improvement target in Fig. 2 is a typical one.) Joint objective setting, however, refers to more than the fact that the objectives which an individual sets are partly "imposed" by others and partly "volunteered" by the individual. It refers also to the facts that the boss assumes responsibility for helping to remove obstacles in the way of the employee, that there is mutual agreement on the priorities of the individual's objectives, that there is agreement on personal development objectives for the employee, and that very often the boss as well as the subordinate may have to "give" a little, especially on the exact method to be used in reaching the objective. Joint objective setting also means coming to an agreement on what went wrong and what went right when the objective is reviewed, and having a mutual willingness to revise, tighten up, drop, or otherwise modify the objective based on the review.

UNIT 2

MBO AND YOUR APPROACH TO MANAGEMENT

When we speak of an objective or a goal we generally mean some desired state of our work, our organization, or our being which is different from what it is now. An objective is the statement of some desired *result*. So, whether we like to think of ourselves as "goal-oriented" or as "results-oriented," we really mean the same thing. And whether we prefer the term MBO or MOR (management by objectives and results) again makes little difference. What is important is that a meaningful objective in the context of MBO recognizes a gap or discrepancy in a situation which we want to close or eliminate, and also makes a commitment to the improvement of that situation. In some cases an objective might be construed as a retreat instead of an advance—for example, to get out of a business or to discontinue a service that has become a drain on the organization's vitality. In any case the ultimate purpose, even in such retrograde movements, is the improvement or upgrading of the organization.

IMPROVE-MENT—THE KEYNOTE

The need for improvement of the organization must be the ultimate source and reason behind every set objective. We may appear to be belaboring this point, but let's put it right up front where it belongs: too many objectives are set simply because "you can't have an MBO program without objectives." In a superficial, noncommital approach to MBO, the most easily set objectives (and those which usually emerge) are simply statements of what the organization or the individual is already focusing on or completing. If this is the type of objective which is set and goes unchallenged, the fate of your MBO system is sealed from the beginning. In fact, these are *non-objectives,* as F.D. Barrett has pointed out:

> **"** *Objectives are not mere verbal statements typed on pieces of paper. They are intentions formed in men's minds — they are visions about what could be accomplished. If there are no intentions, . . .or visions in the manager's mind, there are no objectives. What does not exist, cannot be written.*[1] **"**

Considered in that light, the quality of an objective is a revealing measure of the person who creates it. It indicates the acceptance of the important role managers play in organizational change, and is a direct reflection of the desire to perform the full scope of the management job.

YOUR APPROACH TO MANAGE-MENT

To read about MBO is one thing, but to introduce it into your organization and subject yourself to its demands is something else again. As you have already discovered if you started with Vol. I, MBO is a very demanding system of management. Those who entered it because it was the only way to break through a salary barrier in the organization, or who accepted it (perhaps reluctantly) because they were the best accountant, engineer, or salesperson in the group may still be struggling to develop a philosophy of management which is acceptable to them. Others (regardless of their original reason for entering the management field) may have lost the will to

---

[1]F.D. Barrett, "Everyman's Guide to MBO," *Business Quarterly,* Summer 1973, p. 76.

manage and become satisfied with the status quo. They ride out whatever storms come along in the form of MBO or any other attempts to change the organization. Firmly entrenched in routine detail, these managers typically perform very reluctantly and non-productively in the process of objective setting. Often allowed to exist in suspended animation for a number of years, they feel threatened by and strongly resist thinking in terms of organizational improvement. Only with great patience can one inspire such individuals to start thinking again in terms of improvement and objectives.

Such a situation is clearly an indictment of higher management. Our primary interest in it, however, is as an indication of the person's philosophy or approach to the profession of management. Your personal approach to management will affect your acceptance of the MBO concept, and will be an integral factor in how you tackle the job of installing MBO, spearheading the program, or selling the idea to your manager. Knowledge of the MBO concept is not enough to get the job done.

Your management philosophy is a collection of beliefs, attitudes, values, remembrances of past experience, and other intangibles which help to shape your behavior on the job. Considering its importance, we will pause at this point and give you the opportunity to assess your own philosophy or approach.

Turn to Exercise 2, paying special attention to instruction C. If your responses are biased by what you think *should* be the response, what you think your boss *wants,* or what someone you respect *does,* rather than reflecting what you feel or would tend to do under the circumstances, you are deceiving no one but yourself. Self-analysis is difficult, because self-deception is a natural defense mechanism against damage to the ego. We all indulge in it to some degree, but try to avoid it as you do the exercise.

EXERCISE 2 Instructions:

A. Respond to all the eighty satements by circling the letter combination which most nearly states your reaction:

SA = I strongly agree
TA = I tend to agree
TD = I tend to disagree
SD = I strongly disagree

B. If a statement does not apply to you in your present job (e.g., if you are not a higher-level manager, if you are in a nonbusiness environment, or if you do not have subordinate managers reporting to you) respond to the best of your ability in the way that you would if you were in such a position.

C. Make every effort to reflect your own reactions. *Do not* respond the way you feel you should, or the way you think someone else would. There are no "right" answers.

D. Take all the time you need, and feel free to change your initial response. However, do not discuss the statements with anyone else before you have recorded your final choices.

E. After you have responded to all the statements, *but not before,* turn to page 39 for scoring instructions and an analysis of your scores.

1.	I become uneasy or annoyed when subordinates or group members present ideas which appear to contain unanswered questions.	SA	TA	TD	SD
2.	There is often too much political maneuvering at high management levels for my tastes.	SA	TA	TD	SD
3.	Detail associated with a management job is essential and an important part of the job.	SA	TA	TD	SD
4.	A high-level management job is desirable because it allows the holder the opportunity to be recognized as a leader.	SA	TA	TD	SD
5.	In a management training course, I would much prefer to actively engage in gaming, simulation, and role playing than hear a good lecture.	SA	TA	TD	SD
6.	In a group where there is disagreement I tend to keep my views to myself.	SA	TA	TD	SD
7.	I prefer open healthy competition with my associates to an atmosphere where everyone is mutually helpful and supportive.	SA	TA	TD	SD

8. I feel that the top persons in most organizations really earn their high pay because of the responsibilities placed on them. SA TA TD SD

9. As a manager, one must enjoy the mental stimulation of trying to find errors or inconsistencies in an argument or proposal submitted by subordinates. SA TA TD SD

10. Politics and the use of personal influence have little or no place in the well-run organization. SA TA TD SD

11. Many otherwise soundly conceived projects fail because of top management's lack of concern for detail. SA TA TD SD

12. I feel that the ability to do something different from most people is an important aspect of any job. SA TA TD SD

13. I believe in the ideal of "completed staff work" wherein the manager need only review and approve or dis-approve the course of action recommended by subordinates. SA TA TD SD

14. I am so much disturbed by a leader who is not actively leading a group I am in, that I will usually try to fill the role that the leader is supposed to be filling. SA TA TD SD

15. I would enjoy receiving a promotion more if I knew that I was chosen in a close decision over a top-notch slate of other candidates. SA TA TD SD

16. Most high-level managers owe their success to their decision-making ability and keen minds. SA TA TD SD

17. The best part of a high-level management job is that it insulates one from the confusion of the work that is going on. SA TA TD SD

18. One of the major attractions of a management position is the ability to direct the efforts of other people. SA TA TD SD

19. A high-level manager should not become concerned with minor aspects of any job. SA TA TD SD

20. Higher-level management is a prestigious and satisfying position because it sets a person apart from the crowd. SA TA TD SD

21. I prefer spectator sports viewed on television rather than attending a live event. SA TA TD SD

22. I am likely to remain on the sidelines of a discussion in which I am the lone dissenter even if I feel my views are right. SA TA TD SD

23.	I prefer sports in which I play against the clock or for my own pleasure rather than against other players.	SA	TA	TD	SD
24.	The jobs of most managers who have reached the top require little of them in energy and devotion of personal time.	SA	TA	TD	SD
25.	A high-level manager should spend a good proportion of time getting to know how his or her subordinates think.	SA	TA	TD	SD
26.	I prefer letting my subordinates develop their own ideas and solutions to the approach of proposing solutions for their consideration.	SA	TA	TD	SD
27.	The concern for details of a major management task should be left to subordinates.	SA	TA	TD	SD
28.	I enjoy looking for activities which are unique and distinctive against which I can pit my skills and expertise.	SA	TA	TD	SD
29.	I prefer actively participating in lively games where chance is the determining factor rather than in long-drawn-out games of strategy.	SA	TA	TD	SD
30.	I definitely feel that a majority of my time as a manager should be spent thinking and planning rather than imposing my influence on my people.	SA	TA	TD	SD
31.	Advancement in an organization should be the result of a healthy process of survival of the fittest in a series of of challenging tasks in which many candidates test their abilities.	SA	TA	TD	SD
32.	I respect top managers' opinions because they usually have a broader view of the situation than their subordinates.	SA	TA	TD	SD
33.	I do not enjoy activities such as puzzles, cryptograms, and brain-teasers, which involve getting answers that are elusive.	SA	TA	TD	SD
34.	I try to avoid utilizing the influence of my position to get things done by my subordinates.	SA	TA	TD	SD
35.	A manager should be held accountable if lack of procedures for handling routine matters interferes with the performance of the organization.	SA	TA	TD	SD
36.	There should be no privileges accorded high-level managers in terms of reserved parking spaces, executive washrooms, and similar distinctions.	SA	TA	TD	SD

37. One of the most distasteful parts of the work of a high-level manager is the effort involved in visiting field operations and customers.   SA   TA   TD   SD

38. Top level managers spend too much of their time in group decision making as opposed to making decisions themselves.   SA   TA   TD   SD

39. I feel that the top-managerial practice of surrounding oneself with capable, ambitious lieutenants is very risky for the organization and for the chief executive because of the power struggle that can result.   SA   TA   TD   SD

40. I do not admire the characteristics of most high-level managers that I know.   SA   TA   TD   SD

41. When things go wrong, I am more interested in factual reports from my surbordinates on what happened and what is being done to correct it than I am in conducting postmortems on the ''why's'' and the implications.   SA   TA   TD   SD

42. The knowledge that I am making things happen is the greatest thrill in my job as a manager.   SA   TA   TD   SD

43. When I work overtime it is often to complete essential routine activities which I did not have time to get done during the day.   SA   TA   TD   SD

44. As a top manager, I would be uncomfortable if I entered a room and employees behaved in a manner which tended to mark me as someone special.   SA   TA   TD   SD

45. In a classroom setting, I feel more comfortable listening to a good speaker than I do discussing a case or working with a group.   SA   TA   TD   SD

46. I tend to seek out professional offices, chairmanships, and other off-duty management activities.   SA   TA   TD   SD

47. I feel that a manager is kept on his toes by trying to stay one step ahead of a capable associate, and that such relationships are mutually beneficial.   SA   TA   TD   SD

48. I feel that a widely-recognized and accepted authority figure in an organization is essential to the effective functioning of that organization.   SA   TA   TD   SD

49. A top manager should not hesitate to bypass immediate subordinates and go out into the shop to observe first-hand any situation that is bothering him or her.   SA   TA   TD   SD

50. One of the greatest frustrations of today's leaders is their loss of autonomy and control over their employees.   SA   TA   TD   SD

51. Delegation, while good for employee development, is useful primarily as a way of releasing the manager from details of execution so that he or she can concentrate on longer-range matters.   SA   TA   TD   SD

52. I would get a thrill out of writing a book to make my experience and philosophy of management available to others.   SA   TA   TD   SD

53. The mental effort necessary to prepare a complex technical report or presentation makes it an unsettling and anxiety-producing task.   SA   TA   TD   SD

54. I find the thought of taking on the task of volunteer community leadership distasteful.   SA   TA   TD   SD

55. I feel that a person should try to be the best in whatever task he or she undertakes on or off the job.   SA   TA   TD   SD

56. I feel that a study of the lives of eminent business, political, and military leaders would reveal an alarming picture of self-aggrandizement and desire for personal gain.   SA   TA   TD   SD

57. The way a business or agency is organized probably plays as great a long-range role in its success as the products or services it develops.   SA   TA   TD   SD

58. In communicating with a subordinate by telephone, I strongly prefer to do the calling rather than to be the recipient.   SA   TA   TD   SD

59. I expect my subordinate managers to be fully informed on the current status of programs in their areas.   SA   TA   TD   SD

60. I tend to model my management style after that used by a distinctive but controversial leader such as a Townsend, a Kissinger, or a Meany.   SA   TA   TD   SD

61. I would get much more satisfaction from managing a smooth-running, profitable but fairly stable organization than from managing a new-product business with many problems and near-term losses but with great potential.   SA   TA   TD   SD

62. The healthy desire to assert oneself is an important attribute for a manager to have in my position or in one to which I aspire.   SA   TA   TD   SD

63. The awarding of incentive compensation to the various divisions of a company based on their relative profit contributions more often leads to destructive competition than to improved performance.   SA   TA   TD   SD

64. I would rather pattern my life on a great missionary or philanthropist than on a great business or political leader.   SA   TA   TD   SD

65. A top management which "has it all together" and has a firm sense of direction is the strongest motivator to individual performance at all levels in the organization.   SA   TA   TD   SD

66. In negotiating with another party, one of the great satisfactions is to get the other party to make the first concession.   SA   TA   TD   SD

67. As long as I have the overall picture that things are going well in my operation, I am perfectly satisfied to leave day-to-day matters to my subordinates.   SA   TA   TD   SD

68. Membership in an exclusive club which allows association with the elite is a managerial prerogative which I fully support.   SA   TA   TD   SD

69. Even if the effort proved largely unsuccessful, I would greatly enjoy being involved in trying to put the mathematical techniques of management science to work in my organization.   SA   TA   TD   SD

70. I strongly prefer a conciliatory approach to resolving conflict in my operations to a more direct "head-knocking" approach.   SA   TA   TD   SD

71. I would derive much satisfaction from being among the top three candidates for an important promotion even if I were not selected for it.   SA   TA   TD   SD

72. The problems of our society could be solved much more effectively if more grass roots input and less top-level authority was applied.   SA   TA   TD   SD

73. I do not think that a top-level manager should spend much time touring his facilities and offices to get the feel of the situation.   SA   TA   TD   SD

74. The use of the power which goes with the position is a trap which a high-level manager should avoid falling into at all costs except as a last resort.   SA   TA   TD   SD

75. I am very hard on my subordinate managers when I discover errors of fact or logic in reports and recommendations coming from their operations.   SA   TA   TD   SD

76. The work of a true leader should be quiet, behind-the-scenes, and not such as to attract the favorable attention of the press and the public.   SA   TA   TD   SD

77. One of the worst aspects of a management job is the desk time that has to be spent on it.   SA   TA   TD   SD

78. One of the great satisfactions of management comes when subordinates recognize and solve job problems on their own without involving you.   SA   TA   TD   SD

79. I would enjoy the experience of taking part in a computerized management game simulation where my decision-making skills could be pitted against others.   SA   TA   TD   SD

80. The counterculture movement probably has as its most harmful effect the undermining of public confidence in those in authority.   SA   TA   TD   SD

Scoring Key   Instructions for scoring Exercise 2:

1. An "agree" response is *either* SA or TA. A "disagree" response is *either* TD or SD.

2. For each statement circle the letter which appears in the Score column *only* if your response is the same as that shown in the Response column. (For example, in item 1, circle G if your response was either SA or TA. Do not circle G if your response was either TD or SD.)

3. When you have finished scoring all items, determine the number of times you have circled each letter. This number becomes your score for each of the letters A through H. Enter these numbers in the spaces provided below.

4. Add the eight letter-scores to obtain your *total* score.

5. Turn to the page following the scoring key for an interpretation of the results.

A _____

B _____

C _____

D _____

E _____

F _____

G _____

H _____

Total _____

Statement Number	**Response**	**Score**
1	Agree	G
2	Disagree	D
3	Agree	F
4	Agree	E
5	Agree	H
6	Disagree	C

Statement Number	Response	Score
7	Agree	B
8	Agree	A
9	Agree	G
10	Disagree	D
11	Agree	F
12	Agree	E
13	Disagree	H
14	Agree	C
15	Agree	B
16	Agree	A
17	Disagree	G
18	Agree	D
19	Disagree	F
20	Agree	E
21	Disagree	H
22	Disagree	C
23	Disagree	B
24	Disagree	A
25	Agree	G
26	Disagree	D
27	Disagree	F
28	Agree	E
29	Agree	H
30	Disagree	C
31	Agree	B
32	Agree	A
33	Disagree	G
34	Disagree	D
35	Agree	F
36	Disagree	E
37	Disagree	H
38	Agree	C
39	Disagree	B
40	Disagree	A
41	Disagree	G
42	Agree	D
43	Agree	F

Statement Number	Response	Score
44	Disagree	E
45	Disagree	H
46	Agree	C
47	Agree	B
48	Agree	A
49	Agree	G
50	Agree	D
51	Disagree	F
52	Agree	E
53	Disagree	H
54	Disagree	C
55	Agree	B
56	Disagree	A
57	Agree	G
58	Agree	D
59	Agree	F
60	Agree	E
61	Disagree	H
62	Agree	C
63	Disagree	B
64	Disagree	A
65	Agree	G
66	Agree	D
67	Disagree	F
68	Agree	E
69	Agree	H
70	Disagree	C
71	Agree	B
72	Disagree	A
73	Disagree	G
74	Disagree	D
75	Agree	F
76	Disagree	E
77	Agree	H
78	Disagree	C
79	Agree	B
80	Agree	A

Commentary on Exercise 2

Analyzing your scores This exercise assesses the degree to which you possess each of the eight traits or tendencies believed to be a measure of a person's "motivation to manage." Six have been identified by John B. Miner[1] as:

> The holding of favorable attitudes toward those in positions of authority (scale A)
>
> The desire to engage in competition, especially with peers (scale B)
>
> The desire to assert oneself and take charge (scale C)
>
> The desire to exercise power and authority over others, particularly subordinates (scale D)
>
> The desire to behave in a distinctive way, which involves standing out from the crowd (scale E)
>
> And a sense of responsibility for carrying out the numerous routine duties associated with management (scale F)

To these are added two behavioral tendencies that motivate the managers to take the types of action required to be fully effective. These are:

> The need for *structure*: the desire to make sense of facts, problems, people, or facilities, particularly to have questions and inconsistencies resolved (scale G)
>
> The *"effectance"* need: the desire to engage in stimulating mental and physical activity involving expenditure of energy as opposed to sedentary or passive pursuits (scale H)

High scores on all these eight scales or dimensions of your approach to the management job do not in themselves *predict* management success. But extensive studies of large numbers of managers have resulted in the conclusion that success in accomplishing managerial goals is often associated with a strong competitive drive, a high energy level, and a willingness to spend time on the inevitable drudgery as well as on the exciting aspects of management. Similarly, those who have no desire to lead, fail to assert themselves, have little identification with authority figures or their values, or desire to

---

[1]John B. Miner, *The Human Constraint,* (Washington, D.C.: Bureau of National Affairs, 1974).

remain merely a face in the crowd by not rocking the organizational boat cannot be expected to conquer difficult goals that require the cooperation of others.

Some managers or managerial aspirants may score low on scales C and D (power and assertiveness) because they have been taught to frown upon the exercise of power. In fact, however, *power* is a neutral term meaning only the ability to influence others. No matter how participative the manager's style, his or her actions are always purposeful, and the purpose is normally to influence the subordinate to do a better job in contributing to overall goals. The autocratic use of power can be for "good" ends as well as "bad," and the democratic use of it for "bad" as well as "good." But the use of power remains an essential part of management. If you scored low (less than 4) on scales C and D, go back and reexamine your feelings regarding the use of power, keeping in mind our definition of it as *the ability to influence others.*

Structure is another term that has acquired negative connotations because of the behavioral science principle that giving people freedom and self-control motivates them more than forcing them to operate in a rigidly structured environment. You should recognize immediately the difference in our use of the term. The need to have things make sense — to have all the pieces fit together — is the attribute being measured in this self-analysis. At the same time, this need for structure, unaccompanied by a high effectance (energy) level, can cause the manager to adopt a "set it and forget it" approach — in other words, to become complacent. Likewise, a high energy level without structure can obviously lead to chaos. Therefore, high scores (7 or higher) on both scales G and H are likely to be associated with a productive pattern of managerial behavior.

No paper and pencil test, including this one, can give you all the answers about yourself. You should regard these results not as a characterization of you as a manager, nor as a predictor of success in the field or in leading an MBO program, but simply as a framework within which you can explore your motivation to manage and the modes of behavior which you use to satisfy that motivation.

Note especially that collaboration, as well as competitiveness, is a productive managerial behavior. Likewise, power *redistribution* (delegation) is called for, as well as power *assertion.* In fact, MBO demands a great deal of collaboration between bosses and their subordinates, and requires a highly developed skill in delegation. The important point is that if your drives for competition, power, and assertiveness are not strong, you must be very certain that you compensate for their absence by exercising the skills of mutual objective setting and performance review, which we will help develop in this volume and in Vol. III. These skills will also provide a balance for those whose style may be excessively assertive, competitive, or both.

We make no apologies for appearing to fly in the face of modern behavioral science by recognizing the legitimacy of drives for power and competition. Nor do we apologize for what may seem (later on) to be a tendency to "work both sides of the street" when we espouse many of the principles of behavioral science. We are not trying to remake you as a person, but merely to emphasize a point we made in Unit 1: that a wide range of behavior may be required to realize the full potential of the MBO system. George Odiorne summed it up in referring to the objective-setting process:

> **❝** *It's true that participative management is perfectly acceptable as one method of goal-setting in the MBO system. As a system, however, MBO works also by autocratic or top-down goal-setting. The choice of which method to use, or when to mix them, is determined more by the demands of the situation, especially the expectations of subordinates, than by the basic nature of the system itself.*[2] **❞**

He might have added "the basic nature of the manager" to his determinants, and we would have preferred him to say "how to balance" rather than "when to mix" the methods, but the need for versatile management is clear, as is the need for managers to *choose* and *act*.

---

[2]George S. Odiorne, *Management by Objectives: A System of Managerial Leadership* (New York: Pitman, 1965), p. 140.

UNIT 3

THE OBJECTIVES OF OBJECTIVES
DOCUMENTATION, MEASUREMENT, AND MOTIVATION

Generally speaking, an objective exists for three reasons: (1) to provide a clear, understandable *documentation* of the need for improvement and the commitment made to it, (2) to establish a basis for the *measurement* of performance, and (3) to give positive *motivation* to the performer. An objective that meets all these purposes requires careful preparation. Furthermore, it must be *used* continually throughout its active life by both boss and subordinate, and not merely put in a file. The use of objectives in the performance appraisal process is the subject of Vol. III. In this volume, we are concerned primarily with preparation and validation—the close examination of an objective to determine its realism and quality. First, we will set up some criteria to use in preparing objectives. This will help ensure that your objectives fulfill the three functions we have defined.

OBJECTIVES AS DOCUMEN- TATION

As documentation of the organization's — or the individual's — commitment to improvement in the areas where it is most needed, an objective should meet three requirements in addition to the obvious one that it must be *written*: (1) it should be *supportive* of the parent organization, (2) it should reflect the *most important needs* and contributions of the writer, and (3) it should be *interlocked* with the objectives of other components of the parent organization.

The prerequisite that an objective be written might seem too trivial to dwell upon, except that many employees, reacting to what they see as the excessive formality and paperwork that MBO entails, rebel at having to "write it all down." In fact, life in most organizations is so complicated that written agreements are necessary merely to remember what was decided. Even the "one-person organization" finds it necessary to make notes to itself to provide a record, if only in the form of a tickler on some future page of the calendar pad warning against slippage before it is too late.

The three additional criteria are not so self-evident. However, all three are important to the success of the MBO process itself, since they contribute to the overall unity of direction and effort that provides a large part of MBO's benefits.

The first requires that each objective stand inspection as to the *support* it gives to overall organizational objectives. Figure 2 (see page 9) illustrates how the supportiveness requirement is satisfied at successively lower levels in the organization.

The second states that, to be truly useful, objectives that are recorded and monitored should relate to the *major, top-priority needs* of the organization. A system which requires the documentation of every activity by all participants, no matter how trivial or peripheral, will soon fall of its own weight in paperwork — unnecessary, unread, and unproductive. For example, a foreman's objective to hold a meeting with his crew every other week throughout the year — while it may contribute to improved employee relations (an important area of results for most organizations) — is one best left to informal review by and with the immediate manager as a "maintenance" item. (Unfortunately, the neglect of these maintenance or preventive measures can have serious negative consequences, so that a periodic review of such measures is necessary. In some cases, it might be desirable to obtain a documented commitment to achieve the required improvement — for example, from a foreman who has *not* been performing well in this area.)

The third requirement is that each objective be *interlocked* with those of other organizational components that may be affected by it. Ideally, an objective that is achieved by one component of an organization should not have serious undesirable side effects on another component. This is often an impossible ideal — for example, the development of a new product by the R & D component may result in higher costs in terms of quality and machine turnaround time for the manufacturing component. Nevertheless, the objectives of all affected components should be integrated before they are made final, so that all members of the organization are made aware of the probable effects and can plan to minimize the unfavorable ones. The integrating or interlocking process simply involves horizontal communication with others who may be affected by your objectives, supplementing the vertical communication between you and your boss or subordinate. This is not an appeal for a committee system of decision making, but merely for sufficient interplay among associates to assure adequate information for decision making and conflict resolution.

OBJECTIVES AS MEASUREMENT TOOLS

If an objective is to facilitate the measurement of performance, it must satisfy several additional requirements. We stressed earlier the need for written objectives for the purpose of documentation; now we must emphasize that objectives be written in *measurable terms* if they are to help measure performance. This requirement simply means that an objective must not be stated in terms that are indefinable either qualitatively or quantitatively. Objectives expressed as improvements in morale, employee relations, cooperation, customer relations, corporate image, product acceptance, etc., are qualitatively undefinable, and offer little hope of measuring progress or achievement.

Such objectives can be useful only if they are restated in terms of observed or reported events, incidents, or classifiable behavior involving individuals or components that contribute to or are a part of the quality being measured. For example, an objective to improve morale in the office might be stated in terms of absentee rates, turnover, attendance at social functions, numbers of complaints made to the boss (or to others), numerical ratings obtained on successive employee attitude surveys, or in any other verifiable way that boss and subordinate can agree upon.

Objectives may also be undefinable quantitatively. The most common offense is describing improvement as "considerable," "substantial," or "significant." This is a natural result of stating the objectives qualitatively in undefinable terms. After all, what more precise degree of improvement than "significant" or "substantial" can one ask for when dealing with a nebulous quality like morale or the corporate image? These problems in quantifying the degree of improvement generally disappear when the object of the improvement is clearly defined in terms of measurable or verifiable quantities or events.

With this prerequisite understood, we can define the other requirements for an objective to do its job as a measurement tool. An objective should be (1) *results-oriented* (stated in terms of a desired outcome), (2) *specific* in its scope, (3) *clear* in its intent, and (4) *time-binding* on the writer (subject to deadlines or other time constraints).

The first of these is results orientation. However measurable an objective may be, it may still fall short of providing a meaningful yardstick for measuring results or performance. Unless it is stated in terms of *useful* results, its completion is primarily a measure of activity or "busy-ness." If that activity is not clearly a contribution to some desired result, it may become what George Odiorne calls an "activity trap," a more or less meaningless repetition (often becoming steadily more efficient!) of work which no longer serves a useful purpose.

An example of pure activity in the form of an objective meeting all of the requirements for measurability is this one submitted by a corporate training director:

> ❝ *The Office of Training and Development will increase by 10 percent the number of human relations seminars provided to operating departments in the next fiscal year over the level of 140 projected for the current year, with no increase in personnel.* ❞

Inherently there is nothing wrong with this activity, as long as it is directed at filling real needs and is of the kind and quality which may be expected to do so. *As stated,* however, the objective does not reflect the concern for results and the thought the training director has put into it. A restatement or refinement of the same objective that would reflect the purpose and the results expected might be:

❝ *The Office of Training and Development will increase by 10 percent . . . the number of human relations seminars for the first-line supervisors, designed to reduce the proportion of grievances reaching the second step of the grievance procedure. Anticipated results are increased competence in handling employee problems reflected in a reduction of 20 percent in the number remaining unsettled after the verbal and first written stages.* **❞**

We say more about the issue of results versus activity in the next unit, and in Vol. III when we discuss performance appraisal. Meanwhile, we refer you to the job description shown in Fig. 3. This document defines in measurable terms how the incumbent's performance of each responsibility is to be evaluated. It is a useful guide for establishing objectives that are both measurable and results-oriented.

The second and third requirements, *specificity* and *clarity,* are often overlooked in objective setting. This causes much conflict over such issues as what exactly the subordinate promised to do versus

TITLE:	Manager of Production Engineering	DATE:	2/21/___
DIVISION:	Manufacturing		
RESPONSIBLE TO:	Plant Manager	LOCATION:	Houston

I. Purpose

The manager of production engineering is accountable to the plant manager. The section is responsible for providing and maintaining manufacturing facilities and processes for production of new and existing products at optimum cost and quality levels.

The section is a vital link in the prompt transfer of newly engineered products into full-scale production and is a major contributor to the company's reputation as a responsive, cost-competitive, and quality supplier. It is the company's first line of defense in protecting the safety of employees and customers from the hazards of the production processes and of poorly manufactured products, respectively. It carries primary operating responsibility for the protection and conservation of the impacted environment of the plant.

FIGURE 3
Statement of Position
Scope and Purpose
(pp. 49-53)

II. Position Scope and Responsibilities

A. *Functional and Managerial Responsibilities*

Design and install all processing and handling equipment and other manufacturing facilities for new products, expanded production of existing products, environment control, and general plant improvements.

Provide for design of equipment for the above purposes by utilization of engineering resources outside the section, internal or external to the company, whenever the work involved can be done more economically elsewhere.

Revise and standardize existing processes for improved control and quality of all products, and improve labor and machine utilization upon consultation with the manager of industrial engineering and the plant superintendent.

Reduce manufacturing costs by any of the means above, by improvement of material and energy balances, and by service to the manufacturing section to solve production difficulties.

Introduce into plant operation experimental products in cooperation with the engineering division and manufacturing section.

Provide for all maintenance and safety services to the Houston plant.

Coordinate and compile plant capacity figures periodically and initiate action to provide necessary increases.

Provide estimates of facilities expenditures, manufacturing costs, and other applicable technical data for use by sales and engineering divisions in preliminary evaluations of new products.

Take an active part in plant cost reduction and safety programs, as a member of management.

Maintain an awareness of new technical developments and regulatory requirements within the industry and apply these whenever practicable.

Provide for continuity and growth of plant capability by selecting and developing competent personnel to carry out the work of the section.

B. *Relationship Responsibilities*

Delegate to subordinates the fullest possible measure of authority for decision making and contribution to profits, and provide a climate in which employees may discuss their plans and problems and receive advice and counsel, without relieving them of their decision-making and other operating responsibilities.

Coordinate the resources and efforts of the section with other sections and with the engineering and sales functions by participation in business team and other activities.

Use the functional services and appraisals of staff divisions as their concentration and specialization upon functional aspects enable them to provide such aid.

Make fullest practicable use of informal "channels of contact" to supplement channels shown on the organization chart, and encourage other members of management to do likewise.

III. Position Authority and Reservations of Decision-Making Authority

Standard Practice Instruction PE-4, entitled "Delegation of Authority," establishes reservations of decision-making authority from the manager and subordinates.

The manager has the authority and responsibility to make recommendations as to subject matter on which decision-making authority has been reserved, to secure decisions thereon, and to take appropriate action thereafter.

IV. Criteria and Measures of Performance for the Position

The criteria and measures of successful performance by the manager of production engineering will include the following items.

A. Effectiveness of activities to provide required production facilities for new and existing products, as measured by:

1. Thoroughness of periodic audit of future needs, and changes in effective plant capacity figures
2. Extent of lost business because of late facilities installation*
3. Success of toll production operations when required
4. Reduction of overtime and/or addition of capacity by cycle, utilization, and yield studies*
5. Adherence to engineering and environmental standards of quality in production of new products

B. Effectiveness and timeliness of cost reduction efforts, as measured by:

1. The percentage of actual and budgeted total cost reduction achievement contributed by the production engineering group*
2. Specific improvements in yield, spoilage, manufacturing cycle, and labor and machine utilization obtained through production engineering activities*

3. Reduction in utilities consumption and maintenance costs achieved by engineering improvements*

4. General extent of participation of the group in cost-reduction program activities

5. Long-term trend in planned production cost levels for all products

C. Effectiveness of maintenance and plant engineering services, as outlined in the position responsibilities and measured by:

1. Reduction in machine breakdown time*

2. Effectiveness of cost control against budgets*

3. Performance against established preventive maintenance inspection programs and parts inventory limits*

4. Action in cases of emergency breakdown

5. Coordination of maintenance activities with production schedules

6. Anticipation of need for changes in and additions to utilities and services to the plant

7. Operating difficulties encountered in new equipment, and the effectiveness in elimination

8. Control of costs in connection with plant appropriations

9. Labor and space utilization efficiencies achieved by sound design and drafting

10. Status of labor relations in the maintenance area

[In the original, measures of each of the following criteria were also present. These measures are eliminated here for brevity, but some of them are the subject of Exercise 9, number 5, in Vol. I.]

D. Effectiveness of quality-improvement activities

E. Quality of service provided to other sections and to management, in capital budgeting, production cost estimating, facilities design and layout, and other service responsibilities

F. Effectiveness and extent of participation in professional activities and others involving assimilation and adoption of new engineering knowledge and techniques.

G. Effectiveness of personnel selection and development, including delegation of responsibility and authority

H. Effectiveness of control and use of assigned financial and other available resources in the company

I. Quality and timeliness of decisions and action on all responsibilities, including recommendations where decision-making authority is reserved

J. Thoroughness of hazard analyses conducted on all products and processes, and effectiveness of design work in reducing safety hazards to employees and customers

*Numerical standards of excellence based on current conditions and needs will be set and maintained until revision is indicated. Review will be annual.

what the manager really wanted. Specifying refers in this instance to defining the scope, and clarifying refers to the intent. Take, for example, an objective "to improve labor efficiency by 10 percent." A more specific statement would be "to improve the average efficiency of direct and indirect workers by 10 percent." A further improvement in clarity might be "to improve the average efficiency of direct and indirect workers in terms of output per man-hour of standard products by 10 percent over the average for the preceding 6-month period."

An even more specific and clear statement would be to turn this single objective into two, one specifying a 12 percent improvement for direct workers and the other a 5 percent target for indirect workers. This refinement would be especially helpful since the action plans required to improve output per man-hour in the direct production process will almost certainly be quite different from those needed in the indirect areas.

Obvious? Perhaps—but the original example, without the refinements we have suggested, is typical of the superficial approach taken by many organizations that attempt to implement MBO as painlessly as possible. The utility of the objective, both as a record of intent and commitment and as a yardstick against which to measure progress, improves dramatically as its specificity and clarity are improved.

If you are alert, you have already spotted the failure of all the refinements we have suggested in the preceding paragraphs to conform to our fourth requirement—they are not *time-binding*. None of them clearly specifies a completion date, deadline, or any kind of checkpoint in time. The effect of this glaring omission is obvious: it removes all indications of urgency and priority, and leaves both the employee and the manager open to misunderstanding one another. Was the 10 percent reduction to be applied to the total labor bill for the entire period, or was it a level to be reached at the end of (or at some point during) the period? And what was the period — the next 6 months, the coming year, or. . .?

If action planning is done as we will describe it later in this volume, there must be target dates associated with each step toward the final result. Therefore, an objective without dates immediately raises a suspicion that it has been established without an action plan. Conversely, the presence of a completion date implies that a plan exists. The manager who asks to examine the action plan may find that the date was pulled out of thin air. In either case, the time-binding characteristic of an objective statement provides a check of its validity for both manager and employee.

OBJECTIVES AS MOTIVATORS

The very act of writing out an objective is said by some management authorities to increase the writer's commitment to its completion. There is evidence from a number of experimental studies that just setting an objective provides the motivation to do better. However, other researchers have identified the appraisal and feedback process as the primary motivator. We feel strongly that the whole process of objective setting, monitoring, and feedback provides a definite motivational plus for organizations that use MBO. Still, there are two major requirements we will impose on the setting of the objective that add significantly to its usefulness as a motivator: (1) that it be *jointly set* by the boss and the subordinate and, as a corollary, that the result of that process be fully *accepted* by the subordinate, and (2) that while the objective must represent an improvement, it must be an *achievable* improvement. Two additional requirements for a sound objective that help ensure its achievability are that the person responsible be *supported by the authority* needed to do the job, and that there be a *plan of action* verifying that a method exists for getting it done.

The first requirement (that an objective be jointly set with the participation of the subordinate) provides an added level of commitment to its achievement, because of the generally accepted idea that people who are involved in the creation of a program or decision will work harder to make it a success than people who are not. While not always necessary or sufficient as a positive motivator, the participation of the subordinate in deciding on the objective can be crucial in removing psychological obstacles that could inhibit performance.

The corollary requirement is that the joint product of the objective-setting process be accepted by the subordinate. This will probably be the case if the objective is established in an atmosphere of mutual concern, helpfulness, and negotiation between equals.[1] There can be no real commitment and little positive motivation if the objective is regarded as impossible to achieve or if it is unilaterally imposed against the will (or better judgment) of the subordinate, without regard for his or her capabilities, priorities, or superior knowledge of the job.

Achievability is the second motivational requirement. We stated earlier that an objective which requires only the *present* level of effort, thought, or commitment is devoid of motivation toward improvement. At the same time, too much emphasis in the opposite direction can be equally unmotivating. A highly challenging objective that is perceived by the performer as out of reach because of insufficient time or other resources — or seen only as part of a game because of the lack of real intent on the part of the boss to make it stick — can be ruinous to the whole MBO program.

The achievement-motivated person is stimulated by *moderately* challenging objectives, with the key to motivation being the per-

---

[1]We are not advocating the abolition of the authority structure of the organization, but merely equality in the sense of mutual respect between persons with a common stake in the success of the organization.

Objectives that aim only at present levels of effort miss the target — which is improvement. (© Brilliant Enterprises, 1974)

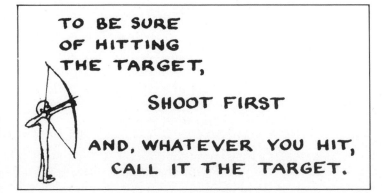

TO BE SURE OF HITTING THE TARGET,

SHOOT FIRST

AND, WHATEVER YOU HIT, CALL IT THE TARGET.

ceived probability of success. The self-motivated achiever is not stimulated by a "piece of cake," but nevertheless wants a reasonable chance to make a significant accomplishment. High achievers are important people in any organization, and an MBO system (if they do not see it as too authoritarian and meddlesome) has the potential to reinforce their achieving tendencies. But whether or not they are high achievers, employees will certainly be turned off by a succession of objective-setting sessions in which it becomes obvious that the product is so much "sound and fury" without the intent or means to make it happen. Disillusionment may not take place immediately, but it is inevitable under such conditions. The final phase is the abandonment of MBO by higher management because the new system does not seem to be producing improved results.

The unachievable objective fails more often because of a lack of needed resources than because the manager or the employee was attempting something entirely beyond reason. The employee may be denied the physical or financial support required or the moral support and accessibility of the manager, or may simply not be delegated the decision-making authority needed to get the job done on time. A clear understanding of his or her limits of authority by every person involved in MBO is a prerequisite for a sound MBO system. A good objective is *supported by the authority needed* to carry it out.

Failure to achieve because of lack of resources is often the result of setting the objective without a fairly precise idea of how it is to be accomplished and what resources are needed. We take the position that an objective is not really complete unless it is *backed up by a plan,* and conclude our list with that requirement. Together with an analysis of the available and required resources, the plan validates the achievability of the objective. This is not to say that the pioneering spirit ("I don't know how I'll do it, but I'll get it done") has no place in the MBO system. But it does mean that this type of objective should be stated in a different way. We will discuss how to handle these "do or die" objectives in Unit 7.

Having read through this rather stringent set of requirements, you may dread the task of setting an objective that meets our standards. It's really not that difficult and will quickly become second nature, if you keep the three purposes — documentation, motivation, and measurement — in mind.

EXERCISE 3   1.   While we could easily propose several statements of objectives for you to criticize, they would test your understanding of only a few of the criteria—specificity, clarity, and time constraint, for example. We do not think that we need to belabor those relatively simple concepts, but at the same time we cannot fabricate statements that everyone would agree are deficient in motivational criteria. Only you know what is realistically achievable in your situation, for instance. It is likewise difficult to synthesize an objective that is clearly deficient in measurability or results orientation. For example, the increase in the number of training seminars that we used as a "bad" example of activity orientation in the text might be interpreted in some organizations as results orientation if the definition of results is "doing what you said you were going to do." (By the way, that's not bad, if you were secure in the knowledge that what you were doing was the *right* thing!)

In any event, we will place the burden on you (a) to find in your organizational or personal plans an objective statement or two, or to formulate one for yourself or your component, (b) to evaluate it critically against all the criteria, and (c) to rewrite it to meet the criteria as fully as you can.

a. Initial Statement

_____

_____

_____

_____

b. Evaluation

Criteria	Rating	What It Lacks
Written?		If you haven't done this, you shouldn't be here. Go back to a!
Supportive of organizational goals?		
Important? (worth monitoring?)		
*Interlocked with other components?		
Measurable?		
Results-oriented?		
Specific?		
Clear?		
Time-binding?		
*Jointly set?		
*Accepted?		
Achievable?		
Supported by authority?		
Backed by an action plan?		

*Skip these if you have written an original objective.

c. Rewrite

_____

_____

_____

_____

2. Suggest several measures that might be established to upgrade the following objectives (taken from the text) for measurability:

Objective	**Measures of Performance**
Improve employee relations	
Upgrade quality of supervision	
Improve corporate image	
Improve customer relations	
Increase product acceptance	

Commentary on Exercise 3

1. This exercise is in most respects a pretest. When you have completed this volume, you may also use it as a post-test. At that time, you should be able to perform this analysis as you think about the objective, so that a rewrite will be in most cases unnecessary. Material that relates to the various criteria is covered in the following units:

Acceptance	Units 8 and 9
Mutuality	Unit 8
Achievability and support	Unit 9
Supplemented by plan	Units 9 and 10
Importance	Unit 4
Supportive and interlocking	Units 4 and 6
Specificity, clarity, and time-constraint	Units 9 and 10
Measurability	Unit 7
Results-orientation	Unit 5

2. Your lists of measures may include the following:

Objective	Measured by
Improved employee relations	man-hours lost in strikes and walkouts
	number of employee grievances
	employee suggestion frequency and value
	number of job applicants referred by employees
	attendance at social functions, open house, etc.
	scores on job satisfaction survey
Improved quality of supervision	number of grievances in unit
	scores on entrance (qualifying) exam
	relative numbers of requests for transfer in versus out, by unit
	percentage performance against schedule
	percentage idle time in unit
	trend in output per man-hour
	percentage machine downtime
Improved corporate image	ratio of favorable to unfavorable editorials
	number of active job applications
	number of employees serving in public or volunteer capacities
	incidence of environmental complaints

	numerical results of public attitude polls
	success ratio in college recruiting
	    (percentage of offers accepted)
	number of requests for public appearances,
	    talks, etc., by employees and managers

Improved customer relations	percentage of repeat orders
	complaint frequency
	delivery performance on emergency orders
	time lag in answering and resolving
	    complaints
	retention of share of customers' orders in
	    downturns
	salespersons' evaluation, by customer

Increased product acceptance	percent market share, by product numerical results of consumer surveys growth rate on new products growth in new applications number of requests for special products number of inquiries resulting from ads, technical articles, etc.

Some of these measures are not specific to the attribute being measured, for example, the trend in output per man-hour may be a result of factors other than improved quality of supervision. This problem, inherent in all measurement, is treated in Vol. III.

Likewise, several are in reality activities, not results; but they may be acceptable because of their undisputed effects — for example, effect of delivery performance on customer relations.

UNIT 4

THE SOURCES OF OBJECTIVES

In the preceding unit we discussed the need for objectives, their fundamental purposes, and the characteristics that any objective must have to fulfill all those functions. However, objectives do no more than reflect the visions and intentions of people. What happens after the objective is written depends to a large extent on the consequences of performing or failing to perform. Equally important, however, are the effort, skills, and judgment put into the action-planning and performance review phases of MBO — subjects covered in the concluding units of this volume and in Vol. III.

Even before objectives are written, the knowledge and judgment used by managers and employees in selecting them are crucial to the success of the system. In Vol. I, we covered the rational process of organizational and personal job analysis that precedes strategy selection and the definition of the organizational mission, emphasizing the range of products or services on which the organization can use its strengths effectively. Only when that process is complete can you set objectives with the full knowledge and judgment necessary.

KEY RESULTS AREAS AGAIN

During the process of organizational analysis we introduced the concept of the key results area (KRA) as a guide for determining what supporting strategies were needed. The list of organizational KRAs was originally proposed by Peter Drucker as a means of determining the multiple objectives of the business firm.

The concept of the KRA is a useful one at all levels of the organization (including the individual), but its major force in directing the overall effort is at the corporate level. The organization's KRAs determine the overall objectives, and these play a dominant role in shaping objectives at all other levels.

KRAs are not brought down from the mountain engraved on tablets of stone. The same type of human judgment involved in selecting objectives is also required to determine the key results areas for an organization, or for a position in it. Drucker's list does, however, serve as a good starting point for most organizations. Although oriented toward a business operation, it can readily be modified or supplemented for use by any other type of endeavor. The areas proposed by Drucker[1] are shown in Table 1 with some of our suggestions for other types of organizations.

Objectives should be selected which have an impact on the results in all of the KRAs. The rationale for this is that the continued neglect of any one KRA can mean serious trouble for the organization or for its mission. (Forecasting the effect of its continued neglect is a good test for determining whether a KRA should be retained on your list.) This does not necessarily mean there must be one objective on your active list for every KRA, because many objectives will have an impact in more than one KRA when achieved. If organizational objectives are short-range (1 year duration or less), there is less

---

[1]Peter F. Drucker, *Management: Tasks, Responsibilities, Practices* (New York: Harper & Row, 1973), p. 100.

	...ucation	Religious
	Curricula	Pastoral care
	Alumni relations, foundation support, grantsmanship	Pledging support, bequests
Physical resources*		
Productivity†		Involvement of congregation
		Ratio of benevolences to operations
Social responsibility*		
Profit requirements	Balance between revenue and expenditures‡	

*Broadly applicable in most classes of organizations.

†Broadly applicable, but less obvious in religious organizations.

‡As restated in this way applicable to all nonprofit enterprises.

danger of neglecting KRAs than when the completion of long-term projects (e.g., 3 to 5 years) make up the objective content. In the latter case, it is easy to lose sight of one or more KRAs, since the same list of objectives is carried over from year to year without review. An annual strategy review, which reassesses the internal climate and the external environment, is the best insurance against important KRAs being ignored, and also against squandering resources in areas that do not need them. Strategy formulation and review is discussed in Vol. I.

FUNCTIONAL KRAS

So far, we have talked about KRAs in their roles as guides for the total organization. However, the concept is equally useful at all levels in finding and selecting objectives. To demonstrate its usefulness, we introduce the idea of *functional* KRAs, so called because they specify the types of contribution that a function of a business (manufacturing, employee relations, finance, etc.) or a city government (planning, public works, fire, police, etc.) should make in furthering the key results areas of the overall organization.

The examples in Table 2 will clarify this concept. You will note that in several cases there may be no continuing major responsibility of staff functions (such as finance and employee relations) to contribute to an organizational KRA (such as marketing). However, staff must be ready to serve when needed, and to develop objectives accordingly. Employee relations might work with major customers in helping them develop a personnel manual (the marketing KRA) or to negotiate a major realignment of the work force with the union (the productivity KRA). Finance might make major contributions to the

Table 2
Organizational KRAs and Supporting Functional KRAs

| Business Function | Organizational KRA | | | |
	Marketing	Human Organization	Productivity	Innovation
Manufacturing	Delivery, performance, quality, new product introduction	Safety, union relations, functional employee development	Functional cost control, machine utilization, labor efficiency	Manufacturing process development
Employee Relations	(Specific contributions as required, such as recruiting a new sales force)	Training and development, union relations, wage and salary administration, recruitment, functional employee development	Functional cost control	Organizational development
Finance	(Specific contributions as required, such as designing an improved incentive compensation plan)	Functional employee development	Functional cost control, information systems, cash management	Management audit

development of an incentive compensation plan for the sales force (marketing KRA) or an employee profit-sharing plan (human organization KRA).

In KRAs such as human organization, all functions should make contributions (such as development of employees within the function). Similarly, cost control by all functions contributes to the productivity or profit KRA, or both. Contributions in the innovation area should be a continuing responsibility of all functions of the organization.

THE MEANS-ENDS CHAIN AS A SOURCE OF OBJECTIVES

We will give you a chance to work with organizational and functional KRAs as sources of objectives in an exercise at the end of this unit. But first we will look at the overall objectives of the organization as the starting point for a chain reaction in formulating objectives that reach down to the lowest levels. This process provides the most frequent source of objectives for all layers of the organization (excluding the top). At successively lower levels it produces more specific and detailed improvement targets, each related to those adjacent to it in the sequence by the *means-ends chain.* In the chain, each objective is an *end* on the level at which it is performed, but it is also a *means* to support an objective at the next higher level of the organization. Figure 4 illustrates this relationship for a single objective, showing how it contributes to the key results area of productivity in a manufacturing firm.

The means-ends chain provides a rich source of objectives for each succeeding lower component of the chain, but it also can result in a proliferation of potential objectives. These can only be kept in control by evaluating the many possibilities in relation to each other and selecting those which represent the most significant contributions.

Proliferation is inevitable in any case, because of the pyramidal shape of the functional organization structure and the increased specialization at the lower levels. This causes a problem of severe information overload if all lower-level objectives are reviewed and monitored at the top level. Therefore, the levels of review must be limited for reasons of time and efficiency. Generally speaking, the distribution of any objective should be limited to the employee committed to it and to his or her immediate manager. The employee's objective becomes incorporated into one of the manager's objectives through the means-end chain. This is not a firm rule, however, since there will always be objectives important enough to warrant review by several levels of management.

Normally, though, this limited distribution rule leaves the major

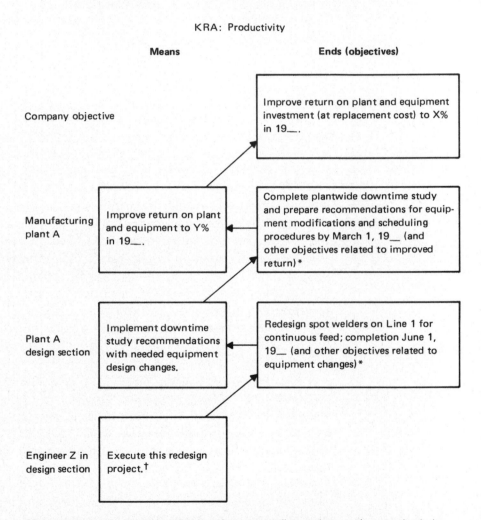

KRA: Productivity

Means   **Ends (objectives)**

Company objective
→ Improve return on plant and equipment investment (at replacement cost) to X% in 19__.

Manufacturing plant A
Improve return on plant and equipment to Y% in 19__.
Complete plantwide downtime study and prepare recommendations for equipment modifications and scheduling procedures by March 1, 19__ (and other objectives related to improved return)*

Plant A design section
Implement downtime study recommendations with needed equipment design changes.
Redesign spot welders on Line 1 for continuous feed; completion June 1, 19__ (and other objectives related to equipment changes)*

Engineer Z in design section
Execute this redesign project.†

FIGURE 4
A means-ends chain— for a comany objective in the key result area of productivity

*Plant A may have many other objectives that can contribute to improved return; the design section may likewise find many other opportunities for equipment change. Finally, Engineer Z may contribute to his section's objectives in many other ways than the one shown here.

†When an objective is so specific that it can be carried out by an individual, such as the design engineer here, it is the end of the chain. That person's ends and means become identical: the achievement of the specific objective.

responsibility for setting and reviewing any objective squarely upon the two people with the largest stake in it. We will discuss the joint objective-setting procedure later in this volume; the review process is covered in Vol. III.

ANALYZING THE JOB ITSELF FOR POTENTIAL OBJECTIVES

Analysis of the job provides a source of objectives in addition to the means-ends chain. The full effort of a component or an individual is not necessarily commandeered by higher management in the support of major programs. Although, strictly speaking, all efforts relate to one or more of the organizational objectives, there is almost always some latitude allowed the individual manager or employee, for example, in determining how to contribute most effectively to overall organizational profit improvement or productivity targets. (In fact, without this latitude much of the self-motivational potential of an MBO system would be lost.) A job description such as the one shown in Fig. 3 facilitates the definition and understanding of the jobholder's potential contributions.

Another way to look at a job (particularly when defining objectives) is to focus on the nature of the activities involved in carrying out its key responsibilities. For this purpose we recommend that the composition of any job be considered a mixture of *continuing, project,* and *unplanned* activities. This "mix" describes the degree of structure in the job, dictates the types of contribution required of the jobholder, and determines the nature of the resulting objectives.

Continuing activities are those directed at maintaining or improving the operations of a business or other organization. They have no end point as long as the particular product or service to which they relate continues to exist. Objectives for these activities are expressed in terms of a level of performance or a standard of excellence. Many jobs in the operating or line functions of an organization are almost entirely made up of these activities (for example, processing loan applications in a bank, or maintaining the quality and productivity levels of a production line in an electronic assembly operation).

Although such jobs are often regarded as routine by the jobholders or their managers, the achievement of significant improvements in performance requires a degree of effort and ingenuity that is far from routine. Unfortunately, routine jobs like these are a haven for those who are interested in maintaining the status quo. As a too-frequent result, many opportunities for innovation are overlooked in the preoccupation with getting the routine job done. We will explore the types of objectives that fit continuing activities in the following unit.

Project activities make up a portion of almost any job. A project is any activity that has an end point marked by the completion of a discrete piece of work — the development of a process, the building of a plant, the selling of a Presidential candidate, the writing of a book, or the closing of a major sales account. Objectives that fit such activities are well known even to those who are not familiar with the MBO system and are usually stated in terms of attainment of the benefits resulting from completion.

In a recent discussion of the applicability of MBO,[2] authority Henry Mintzberg is quoted as recommending MBO only in bureaucratic or divisional (production) organizations and not in the "adhoc-racy" represented by the project-oriented organization. In fact, however, project management would be impossible without the completion objective, which is applied at every stage of the work and at every level of the project organization.

Even in the research organization, where the admonition "You can't schedule inventions" has become a cliché, objectives can be set in terms of areas to be explored, innovative approaches to be followed, and criteria by which progress is to be measured and abandonment decisions made. Objectives like this will help prevent the researcher from becoming mesmerized by a single idea, pursuing it to exhaustion without regard for time and other resources. In short, the project activities in any job are a fruitful source of objectives.

Unplanned activities consist of the unpredictable demands placed upon the job — by the nature of the work itself, by external influences, or both — usually at the expense of the continuing and project activities that the employee has planned. The objectives arising from this type of activity are often directed toward the *elimination* of it, or, if it is an unavoidable part of the job, toward minimizing its unfavorable impact on other activities or facilitating the handling of crises, emergencies, or interruptions.

---

[2]"Perhaps It's Time to Check Out Your Organization's Structure," *Training,* vol. 14, no. 5, pp. 48-50, May 1977.

**ORGANIZA-
TIONAL
PROBLEMS
AND OPPOR-
TUNITIES**

We will return to job analysis and the objective-finding process in the next unit. But to conclude this broad look at sources of objectives, we will turn to organizational analysis as a final method. KRAs and the means-ends chain give a great deal of direction to an organizational component's attempt to set objectives, but the final, specific contributions are determined within the component. Job analysis guides the individual in selecting the contributions he or she can make. Organizational analysis can call attention to improvement needs that none of the other methods reveals. One approach we recommend consists of a comparison of the organization with an ideal. Exercise 4, (4.) contains a structured comparison of this kind based on the organizational improvement potential of an MBO system. You may use it to generate objectives for your component independent of MBO considerations, or to provide specific objectives for your MBO program per se.

Take time to explore the four sources of objectives as they apply to your own job, component, or organization by completing Exercise 4. Use KRAs, the means-ends chain, analysis of your job or mission, and comparison of your organization with the ideal to get an idea of their usefulness in stimulating your thinking about the need for improvement.

EXERCISE 4   1.   Using the KRAs listed, and any others that are appropriate (see Table 1 for suggestions), generate one objective statement, recalling the criteria presented in Unit 3.

KRA	Objective Statement
Innovation	
Human Organization	
Productivity	
Other:	
Other:	

2. a. Complete the means-ends chain shown below, working in both directions, from your boss's level, as indicated, developing objectives which are appropriate to the situation. The boss is the corporate level human resources vice-president. You are the training director.

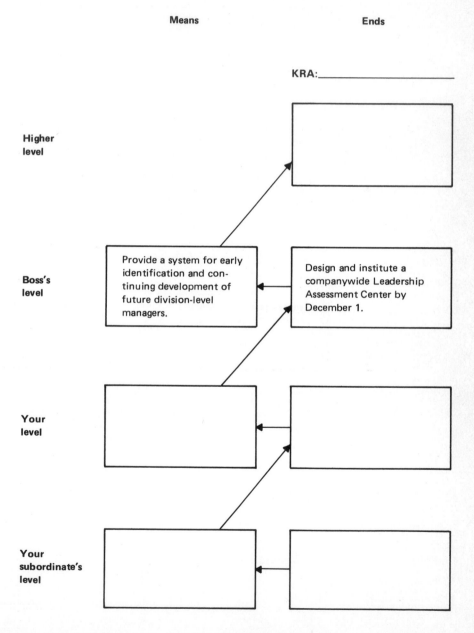

Means

Ends

KRA:_____

Higher level

Boss's level

Provide a system for early identification and continuing development of future division-level managers.

Design and institute a companywide Leadership Assessment Center by December 1.

Your level

Your subordinate's level

b. List several other related objectives which the boss might have added to his ends:

3. List an activity that is typical of each of the three types—continuing, project, and unplanned—as you experience them in your job or component. Write an objective for yourself or your component relating to each.

Activity Type	Specific Activity	Objective
Continuing		
Project		
Unplanned		

4. Diagnose the need for organizational improvement objectives. Rate your organization on a scale of 0 to 10 on each of the following twenty diagnostic questions. Suggest objectives in those areas where you think there are serious weaknesses.

    a. Can each professional (and managerial) employee tell you clearly, precisely, and convincingly why his or her (and each subordinate's) job exists?

    rarely  in all cases

    ### Suggested objective:

    b. Is the rationale for zero-base budgeting understood and accepted?

    not known
    or meets   0 —————————— 10   generally accepted
    with cynicism   and understood

    ### Suggested objective:

c. What types of results does the performance appraisal process produce?

a waste · 0 _____ 10 · extremely useful
of time · · · · · · · · · · · · to management
· · and employees

Suggested objective:

d. Can each manager or employee identify the project or activity which can be picked up during a slack period or when one is forced to put down the present task?

unpredictable
(crisis or higher · 0 _____ 10 · priorities well
management · · · · · · · · · · · · established
dictates) · · and followed

Suggested objective:

e. How does management evaluate the performance of its staff functions?

impossible   0 _____ 10   results clearly
to evaluate   identifiable

Suggested objective:

f. To what extent have results in staff areas improved (declined) in the last two years?

don't   0 _____ 10   trends are
know   closely monitored

Suggested objective:

g. Can each employee identify his or her own training needs and why each is important to the organization?

no, or   0   10   we pursue
don't know   active individual
                                                            development plans

Suggested objective:

h. Are the best talent and adequate financial support being allocated to the most important targets?

don't know   0   10   both are focused
or   and concentrated
disagree   on a few major
                                                            objectives

Suggested objective:

i. What is the justification being used to retain unprofitable products or services?

```
    little                                          anticipation of
    thought     0 _____ 10       future benefits
    given                                            (reviewed every 6
                                                     months for possible
                                                     elimination)
```

Suggested objective:

j. How well do the manufacturing and marketing operations work together on new product introduction?

```
     little
  cooperation,   0 _____ 10      as a team,
     often                                           toward common
  antagonism                                         goals
```

Suggested objective:

k. What procedure is followed to drop or cancel a project or program that ceases to show promise or contribution?

no procedure,   0   10   procedure clearly
mainly continued   defined and
by advocacy   followed

Suggested objective:

l. If funding for development or operations were cut by 10 percent, what activities or personnel would be disengaged?

little   0   10   clearly
thought   identified
given

Suggested objective:

m. Which key people in the organization can normally be counted upon to set tight standards? To overcommit? To hold back?

no basis for judging 0 —————————— 10 each manager knows and works with subordinates on this

Suggested objective:

n. Can our current level of overall performance be traced to specific areas of organizational strength (or weakness)?

little thought given 0 —————————— 10 clearly identified

Suggested objective:

o. Are resources being allocated to the areas of strength? Are corrective efforts or management's attention focused on areas of weakness?

no plans   0 —————————————— 10   appropriate plans
                                          made and action
                                          being taken

Suggested objective:

p. Are high performers in the organization rewarded significantly differently from the average? Are low performers?

not identified,   0 —————————————— 10   compensation
or all   tied to
treated alike   performance

Suggested objective:

q. Does each manager or professional know what his or her level of performance is?

have not discussed it; don't know — 0 .... 10 — yes; by both compensation and other feedback

Suggested objective:

r. How frequently do the ideas of lower and middle management and professional personnel result in changes in top management thinking?

seldom; little credit given — 0 .... 10 — often; ideas are sought, valued, and rewarded

Suggested objective:

s. To what degree have performance standards been tightened in the
   past 3 years for production or line operations? Staff operations?

no change,   0 ————————————————— 10   tightened
accept current   and
performance   achieved

Suggested objective:

t. To what extent is organizational success measured in terms of
   results, rather than *activity* per se?

few measure-   0 ————————————————— 10   as much as
ments used   possible; looking
except in   for better
production   ways
areas

Suggested objective:

Commentary on Exercise 4

1. By this time you have probably noticed that KRAs bear a very close relationship to objectives. In fact, all that is needed to convert a KRA into an objective of sorts is to precede it by the infinitive "to improve." However, don't be trapped by this easy way out. Your objectives should meet the requirements we covered in Unit 3.

    At the lower levels of an organization, particularly in the case of sub-functions that make up a major function such as marketing, KRAs tend to become the names of organizational components—for example, customer relations. (In fact, marketing itself is one of Drucker's generalized KRAs.)

    We hope that the close relationships among these various terms are not creating obstacles to your understanding. The true value of the KRA is in stimulating thought about improvement objectives that have the required characteristics of *good* objectives. The fact that an organizational component bears the same name as a KRA merely indicates the importance of that KRA in structuring the work of the organization and concentrating on the important areas.

2. Similarly, the *means* in a means-ends chain bear a strong resemblance to objectives; in fact, they *are* objectives. Their usefulness to a component, considering the ways the component can contribute to a higher-level end or objective, lies in the stimulation of further search for for and specification of objectives. Refer to Fig. 4 and examine the stated means that the design section contributes to the Plant A downtime objective: "Implement downtime study recommendations with needed equipment changes." This precipitated some immediate work on the spot welders, but also stimulated the setting of other objectives relating to downtime reduction (not specified in the figure). In addition, it led to some innovative thinking about ways (other than downtime reduction) to contribute to the overall plant effort on investment return.

    In the exercise example, the boss's end is sufficiently specific that your means could well be the execution of the Assessment Center project. If you were to keep this project as your own, this would end the chain, as in the case of the engineer in Fig. 4. However, it would be better to subdivide a major objective like this one into several phases. For example, your first end might be to decide upon the form and content of the assessment process. Your subordinate's means might then be to provide you with necessary information; appropriate ends or objectives should follow easily from that point.

3. Refer to the brief description of the objectives appropriate to the three types of activity (starting on page 69) to see if you have recognized the opportunities available. Again, evaluate the quality of your objectives by reviewing the characteristics covered in Unit 3.

4. The positions of your responses on a scale of 0 to 10 to the questions probably represent a mixture of your objective judgment about the facts of the situation and your subjective degree of satisfaction (or dissatisfaction) with the way things are. In either case, responses that you have placed in the lower half of the scales will help focus your investigation of the need for improvement in your organization. These "unsatisfactory" responses represent fertile ground for the establishment of objectives.

The twenty questions are designed to measure the presence of critical attributes which the well-designed MBO system can provide to an organization. Therefore, the degree to which the answers are unsatisfactory is also a direct measure of the need for MBO. Any questions for which the answers are unknown (especially if you are the manager of the component) should give you concern. It is impossible to relate the results of this questionnaire quantitatively to the need for action. A high degree of dissatisfaction in only one area may by itself reflect a critical need for organizational improvement. It is not likely, however, that you have only *one* answer that is unsatisfactory, since it is a characteristic of organizations that problems in one area will create readily perceived symptoms of distress in others.

Record your own comments on the areas needing improvement, for later use. A good way to get validation and confirmation of your individual concerns is to discuss the results of this exercise with others in your organization. The *Leader's Manual* accompanying this series contains exercises for that purpose.

Comments on areas needing greatest improvement

UNIT 5
THE MANY FACES OF OBJECTIVES

Once they are aware of the sources of objectives, as discussed in the preceding unit, most readers will find that ideas flow freely and improvement needs are easily identified in almost any situation. Nevertheless, it may be helpful to expand on our characterization of a job as a mixture of *continuing, project,* and *unplanned* activities. First we will look at a few of the typical needs for improvement in each of these areas, then consider appropriate ways to express the objectives, and, finally, give some examples of objectives which result from this analysis.

CONTINUING ACTIVITIES Continuing responsibilities — for example, keeping costs under control, maintaining the physical plant in running order, processing the never-ending flow of insurance claims, or keeping the city streets in good repair—are a part of most jobs. These may be the *total* responsibility of some jobs, even those of managers and professionals. But even persons who are engaged in highly sophisticated or innovative project work have a certain amount of routine or continuing duties and responsibilities. Creative scientists, for example, must be concerned with the procurement of equipment and supplies, and are often responsible for monitoring their project expenditures. Administrative detail intrudes on even the most free-wheeling entrepreneur and is a thorn in the side of anyone who feels that there are more interesting and important things to be done. This suggests the need to explore opportunities for reducing the amount of time devoted to such activities. When an improvement need of this type is identified, a potential objective is created.

Managers who administer continuing or repetitive activities have another built-in source of objectives—those designed to maintain productivity, interest, and employee growth in the face of boredom and the threat of anomie (the "blue collar blues" or "white collar willies"). Since this should be a continuing concern, we will include it as another source of improvement needs.

Engineers and technicians whose jobs consist of continually upgrading the effectiveness of an operation or of maintaining it in trouble-free operation are also carrying out continuing activities as defined. This is true even though the work may be intellectually demanding and of a high creative content. The objectives for people in such jobs are usually expressed as a desired level of performance or a standard of excellence. As we have indicated, such objectives are incomplete without a back-up plan—a concrete indication of how the desired level can be reached. These plans evolve into projects, each one contributing its share of progress toward the objective.

Specific action plans are always needed to improve the level of performance of a continuous activity. But it is not always necessary to document these supporting plans, especially when they represent numerous small efforts. Documenting such efforts would only clutter the objective-setting process and add excessive paperwork. These plans can usually be a matter of informal agreement between the boss and the employee. They may consist of an increased level of ongoing routine effort, a more intensive application of known principles or methods, or a more effective use of available resources. Although such plans collectively represent a major potential contribution, the most effective way for the manager and the employee to monitor them is to concentrate on their overall *effect* in terms of progress toward the standard or level of excellence required.

Some examples of typical objectives resulting from continuing (and other) job activities are shown in Table 3.

Table 3
Selection of Objectives Based on Job Activities

Job Activity Type	Typical Needs for Improvement	Appropriate Ways to Express an Objective	Examples of Objective/Plan Statements
Continuing	Improved level of effectiveness or performance	Level of excellence or standard of performance	Increase level of on-time deliveries of service by 9/1 to 90% from current level of 82.6%.
		Innovative* program	Based on results of above, prepare plan for reaching long-range goal of 95% for review by manager no later than 12/1.
	Need to reduce time spent	Problem-solving* or innovative program	1. Develop plan for reducing time per unit inspected by 20% (without sacrificing assured quality level) by 6/1.
			2. Implement above plan by 9/1.
			3. Review results and determine further improvement needs and opportunities by 3/1.
	Eliminate or reduce employee boredom	Problem-solving* program	1. Enrich drafting job to include liaison with shop on drafting errors by 5/1.
			2. Get approval from chief by 6/1.
			3. Select six draftsmen and initiate 6-month trial by 8/1.
		Innovative* program	1. Select group to brainstorm the boredom problem (causes and solutions) by next Friday.
			2. Conduct brainstorming session the following week.
			3. Evaluate alternatives and establish priority action plans for all nondrafting areas by end of month.
			4. Conduct employee attitude survey to get "morale base point" also by end of month.

*The distinction between "problem-solving" and "innovative" programs is a fine one. In general, the former refers to the use of known solutions to restore or attain a satisfactory status. The latter implies the generation of new ideas, the attainment of new levels of performance, or both.

Table 3
Selection of Objectives Based on Job Activities *(Continued)*

Job Activity Type	Typical Needs for Improvement	Appropriate Ways to Express an Objective	Examples of Objective/Plan Statements
	Control cost overruns	Level of excellence	1. Obtain agreement from Accounting on new monthly report of overruns by project, by category, at end of this month. Target date for first report is end of next month.
			2. Inform all project directors of new target on overruns (minimum of 90 % of allocated contingency money will be returned unspent to general fund upon completion of each project) by end of next week in group meeting.
			3. Monitor and take corrective action as required on a continuing basis. Review with manager quarterly.
Project	Timely completion	Adjustment of existing objectives, reallocation of resources	Complete Phase III of project 1002 by 7/1 (instead of 8/1 as indicated on tracking chart).
			Overcome slippage in project 301 by increased allocation of effort, and have back on target within 3 months.
	Facilitate needed work	Acceptance or approval as a criterion	Report will be accepted by Board by 9/1 with approval to proceed with major recommendations.
	Assure desired results	Performance criterion	Plant will be running at 100 % of designed production capacity at or below targeted production cost levels within 4 months of initial starting runs.
	Improved method or procedure	Innovative program	1. Review literature on performance appraisal theory and practice — complete 5/15.
			2. Complete survey of firms using the most promising systems by 7/1.
			3. Present proposed system for review by company human resources committee by 8/15.
			4. Complete managerial training seminars in all six divisions by 12/1.
			5. Monitor system during first year of operation.

Table 3
Selection of Objectives Based on Job Activities *(Continued)*

Job Activity Type	Typical Needs for Improvement	Appropriate Ways to Express an Objective	Examples of Objective/Plan Statements

Crisis or Emergency	Cut down on time allotted	Standard of performance with problem-solving or innovative program backup	1. Complete search for equipment and methods to aid in reducing number of false alarms by at least 50%.
			   a. Survey of equipment manufacturers to be completed by 4/1.
			   b. Survey of departments in New York City, Richmond, Atlanta, and Kansas City to be completed by 5/1.
			2. Recommend action program to chief by 6/1.

	Handle crises more effectively	Innovative or problem-solving program	1. Complete analysis of nature, frequency, and importance of crises for patterns of recurrence, by 3/1. 2. Meet with subordinate managers to assign priorities to the problems by 3/15. 3. Assign "top three" recurring crises to McPherson, Jones, and Martinez respectively, to prepare proposals for handling more effectively. Assign by 4/1, for review on 5/15.
	Handle inquiries and complaints for more effective response	Innovative or problem-solving program	1. Mail leaflet describing Listening Post with water bills, 6/15. 2. Advertise Listening Post telephone number and concept in all local papers and radio stations. Complete campaign by 6/28. 3. Recruit person for Listening Post position by 7/1.
		Standard of performance	Give increased attention to customer complaints such that an acknowledgment letter (out-of-town customers) or telephone call (in-town) is sent within 2 working days in every case. Implement immediately.

**PROJECT
ACTIVITIES**
Most jobs, even those in which responsibilities are largely continuing or routine, contain an element of *project* work: one-time activities having a specific purpose or end point and a measurable result. Often, the measurement is in terms of progress toward a desired level of performance. When the effort is of longer duration than a few days, or involves commitment of large amounts of physical and financial resources and depends on a series of interdependent sequential or concurrent steps, the project itself must be monitored. The objective is usually expressed in terms of acceptable and timely *completion.* The measure of acceptability depends on the situation, but timely completion alone does not fully satisfy the results-oriented requirement of a good objective, as described in Unit 3. Completion dates are very important in project work, but it is unthinkable that any major project could be started without performance criteria. However, performance measures do become lost in the shuffle when deadlines approach. The objective statement should include the qualitative performance criteria, and generating plans to achieve them should be part of the objective-setting process. More time spent on establishing and evaluating performance criteria and considering alternative ways to reach the goals set will generally be a good investment in improved results. We will say more about project planning in Unit 10.

For now, let's briefly consider some of the typical needs for improvement in project-type job activities. Acceleration of project work that is falling behind schedule is a continual need. Adjustment of existing objectives and reallocation of resources among projects are common methods for expressing new objectives in such cases.

Preventing cost overruns is another common problem; so common that we categorize this responsibility as continuing in Table 3, and express the improvement objective as a standard of continuing performance. In addition, we specify the measurement tools you may need to implement the objective and the follow-up program to monitor it.

A major class of project-type activities consists of reports, proposals, requests for authorization, and other written documents designed primarily to initiate or facilitate the progress of more substantial work — for example, to get the order, to convince the board of directors that an investment should be made, to get legislative approval for a new program, or simply to maintain the support of higher management for an ongoing program. Here the objective must be more than mere completion. The immediate purpose is to gain approval or acceptance, and the objective must be stated in those terms.

A performance criterion itself may be used as an objective for the start-up phase of a completed project whether the project is a new check-processing facility in a bank, a chemical plant using a new process, a sewage disposal plant expansion, or a new system for processing veterans' benefit payments.

The development of a new machine, process, system, or procedure inspired by whatever need (competitive pressure, cost inflation, quality deficiency, or legislative action) is the most familiar type of objective resulting from project responsibilities. Potentially, it is also the most complex. Such an objective, although it is likely to be stated summarily as a completion objective in conformance with schedules, costs, and performance specifications, may actually consist of hundreds of intermediate, contributing objectives (or milestones) involving many individuals or organizational components. Every major defense system procurement of the NASA mission falls in this category. Sophisticated techniques of project management have been developed to handle these situations, and we have confined our examples in Table 3 to projects of a limited scope which would be executed by an individual or a single component, deferring our treatment of more complex project planning until Unit 10.

UNPLANNED ACTIVITIES Unplanned activities exist in any job. Changing conditions, plans, and priorities, and the fact that even predictable repetitive events do not always occur at a steady predictable pace sometimes conspire to turn even the most routine, programmed job into a nightmare of emergencies, interruptions, and other plan-shattering occurrences. As a result, many employees express frustration and cynicism when the subject of MBO (or planning in any form) arises. Negative as that reaction may be, the state of utter hopelessness that uncertainty induces in many people is even worse.

Continued uncertainty is intolerable to most employees, and many of them use stoic fatalism as a coping mechanism. This is a serious problem for any manager trying to implement MBO, and signals that objectives are long overdue. It is especially important that new managers who find themselves faced with this situation discipline themselves from the start to think of getting off the treadmill.

The unplanned content of the job is a fruitful source of objectives, whether they are initiated by employee or manager. For example, objectives could include cutting down on the time spent handling recurrent crises, dealing more effectively with interruptions, maintaining essential services during emergencies, and so on. These are worthwhile objectives even for jobs that exist specifically to handle unpredictable events.

The objectives in the unplanned area are often expressed in terms of a level of desired performance, such as a reduction in the percentage of time spent handling interruptions, or a decrease in response time for customer complaints. However, many major improvements will require supporting objectives (in the form of specific action programs) to contribute to the attainment of the new level. See Table 3 for examples.

EXPRESSING OBJECTIVES

Throughout this discussion (and in the third column of Table 3) we have tried to boil down the various types of objective statements into a simple classification system. We have isolated two basic types of objectives:

1. Those of a *continuing* nature, expressed as an ever-increasing standard of performance to some ultimate level of excellence. We will call these *type 1* objectives.
2. Those expressed as the *completion* of a program, project, or other discrete activity with an end point and a desired result. We will call these *type 2* objectives. The completed result is often a contribution toward a level of performance expressed as a type 1 objective.

The type 1 objective can stand alone, as noted in our discussions of continuing activities, if it requires no major programs to accomplish it, but generally a type 1 must be backed up by one or more type 2s. Herein lies a potential semantic problem, because one might call a type 2 that supports a type 1 a plan rather than an objective. We prefer our terminology since it recognizes that the implementation plan is in most cases an integral part of the objective-setting progress, and it helps avoid the pitfalls that open up when we decide to "set objectives now and plan later."

The standard of performance is often an interim level leading to the ultimate level of excellence. But the two levels may coincide if the ultimate is within reach during the period covered by the plan, or if the ultimate has been imposed by legislative action or some other source requiring an immediate quantum leap to that level. Examples of the latter are legislated completion dates for pollution abatement facilities or for minimum auto gas mileage standards.

Often, it is relatively easy to achieve some interim standard without an implementation agreement in the form of type 2 objectives, but the ultimate will always require some type 2 support. If it doesn't, you have probably not set high enough levels of excellence. In some cases, though, an *optimum* level of performance may exist beyond which it doesn't make good sense to advance. The quality level of a product or service is an example. You should do a cost-benefit analysis whenever there appears to be an opportunity for improvement that may exceed competitive capabilities or customer expectations and needs. This is especially important when a substantial amount of time or other resources is required to achieve it.

The programmatic type 2 objectives are further divided, as shown in Table 3, into two subclasses: problem-solving programs and innovative programs. As viewed by George Odiorne, the former responds to the organization's need to be able to correct itself or to get back on the track. The innovative program responds to the organizational need for growth and adaptiveness to the changing environment. (You may require separate techniques for developing the action plans to achieve problem-solving and innovative objectives. We discuss these techniques in Unit 10.)

The distinction becomes useful when you're determining priorities among a number of objectives. In many situations, putting the organization back on the track must carry a higher priority than growth. There are many unhappy case histories of firms which grew innovatively only to find that the base on which they built was unstable. Invariably, when they divest or retrench, these companies concentrate on what should have been their top-priority items in the first place — problem-solving programs.

BUT WHAT ABOUT EMPLOYEE DEVELOP-MENT?

You may have questioned the omission of *self-development* and *employee-development* objectives from the foregoing discussion and from the examples shown in Table 3 (except for the performance appraisal development project — a corporate staff technical effort). We recognize this kind of activity as extremely important and as an inherent part of an individual's (or manager's) continuing responsibilities to self (or to employees). But we have deferred discussing it until Unit 7, when we deal with the special case of the manager's own objectives, reflecting (as they should) the major management responsibility for human resource development. Further, the joint process of employee development and its part in the appraisal of performance and potential is treated at considerable length in Vol. III, which is devoted to the performance appraisal process. Meanwhile, we ask that you do a little thinking about employee development in the following exercise.

EXERCISE 5   1. Using Table 3 as a model, identify a need (in your own job) in each of the three areas of activity and an appropriate way of expressing an objective. Then, formulate the objective.

Activity Type	Need	Objective Expressed as	Objective Statement
Continuing			
Project			
Unplanned			

2. In the text, we discussed personal and employee development as improvement needs in the continuing and project activity areas, and therefore as sources of objectives. Write one objective statement (and supporting plan if needed) in each of the spaces below:

Activity	Need	Objective Expressed as	Objective
Self-Development	Presently unable to evaluate proposals and recommendations re computerization and systems revision to my own satisfaction	Problem-solving program	
Employee Development	Eventual need for replacements for self and subordinate managers	Standard of performance	

Commentary on Exercise 5

1. For this exercise we find ourselves unable to predict your responses clearly enough to make a helpful commentary on them. So, we ask you to compare them with a set of responses that you made earlier without benefit of the material covered in this unit.

   Look at your responses to Exercise 4, (3.) and compare the two sets for (1) the quality of the objectives and (2) the relative ease with which you identified them.

2. Your self-development objectives might have taken one of the forms included in the following lists. Congratulations if you backed up the type 1 employee and self-development objectives with type 2s!

Self-Development

Take a short course or attend a seminar.

Delegate review of proposals to a qualified associate.

Execute retainer agreement with a consultant.

Require new format of presentations and/or written proposals designed to answer your questions more clearly.

Complete a programmed instruction manual on the subject.

Employee Development

Performance standard acceptable when each potential opening is backed up with minimum of two persons, with at least one from your own component.

All persons in component have a career development plan prepared and under annual review by manager. Roster of top potential candidates is up to date.

Reach level of at least one management development activity per year for each potential candidate in component.

All temporary absences of manager of more than 3 days' duration are covered by a potential manager, with formal delegation of authority in effect.

UNIT 6

WHY OBJECTIVES FAIL
SOME COMMON PITFALLS

Objectives are the primary tools used in managing by the MBO system. They function as evidence of the contract between employer and employee, as motivators, and as the measuring device for managerial control and employee self-control. But they are *only* tools. The prime movers are the managers, and in their commitment to the process and their skill in selection (and use) of the tools lies the key to success.

Lack of managers' commitment to the MBO process is the overriding and most frequent cause of failure. This commitment is a prerequisite to the effective use of objectives as monitoring and feedback devices. Using them for maximum benefit means spending a lot of time and effort on the measurement process, which is not likely to happen if the commitment is not there.

Poor selection of objectives (usually because of *wrongly assigned priorities*) is another major cause of failure, often complicated by the selection and monitoring of *too many* objectives (and by the prevalent but mistaken notion that all must be monitored at all levels). Proliferation of objectives is likely to lead to *overextending* the available resources of the individual or the organization, another major source of failure.

Lack of skill in formulating the objective statement plan is an obvious problem, and the one that we are most concerned with in this book. Up to this point we have concentrated on the design of objectives. Now we digress from the mechanics long enough to alert you to the problems that can arise from misuse of objectives, no matter how well designed they are. In the next units, we will continue with our treatment of special-purpose objectives, validation, the one-on-one mutual objective-setting process, and preparation of type 2 objectives (or supporting plans, if you prefer that terminology).

MANAGERS' CHOICE: THE LEVEL OF COMMITMENT

We have pointed the finger at lack of management commitment as a major reason why objectives fail to fulfill their potential. Not that we are accusing managers as a class of being uncommitted to their work — the time, energy, and thought that this group devotes to its collective task is evidence that such an accusation is without merit. Furthermore, it would not hold water to argue that managers are not committed to managing *by objectives*. All good managers do this, even if they don't use the term. The problem is that the major project of the moment commands so much of top management's attention — whether the objective be the completion of a merger or divestiture, the negotiation of a securities issue, or the kickoff of a major new product — that its commitment to organizational improvement at all levels is necessarily diluted.

Top management's commitment is translated into concern at lower levels via the chain of command — by the standards set and the value judgments and demands made by each level for those reporting to it. Too often lower-level personnel are not aware of top management's concern for improvement in routine operations, the handling of crises, complaints, grievances, and other mundane aspects of the organization. When this happens, organizational improvement becomes a matter of chance, depending on middle managers' individual motivation to manage (see Exercise 2) or employees' drives for achievement or recognition.

Such random effort does serve to carry the day for many organizations, but it naturally results in less than optimum use of the firm's total human resources. It also throws more than its fair share of the burden for success on the top-level managers, who often must resort to heroic measures (including radical surgery) to keep the organization healthy. The objectives remain those of the executive suite, and what passes down the means-ends chain is only the supportive effort for top management projects. But until economic disaster strikes and top management's objective becomes "slash salaried payroll by 15 percent," these objectives are rarely concerned with organizational excellence (demanding the best efforts and greatest creativity of the whole work force).

In summary, organizational success is too often left to chance—that is, to the degree of self-motivation on the part of employees at all levels—and to the entrepreneurship of a few top managers.

Another kind of noncommitment exists that can be equally harmful to the MBO effort. This is the kind that characterizes the faddist, who eagerly embraces MBO (or any other publicized system), not because he or she is committed to improvement, but in the hope that finally something has come along that will make it easier to manage the business. This manager soon gives up, and another "failure" of MBO enters the record book. Occasionally, one who is more persistent will continue to search the field of MBO consultants, hoping to find a version that will be less demanding. For example, during a recent preliminary discussion of a consulting arrangement we found that the organization had had several previous exposures to MBO, but had made little progress. The trend of the conversation led us to suspect that the problem was a low level of commitment, rather than a poor choice of consultants. This was confirmed when a highly placed manager in the organization asked, "Can you possibly *call* this program something else besides 'MBO'? Our managers have been so overwhelmed with the extra work required by MBO that they probably won't listen to you if you use that name." Believing firmly that there is no *easy* way to introduce MBO effectively, we abruptly terminated the consulting arrangement at that point.

THE HARD WORK OF MONITORING RESULTS Most managers subscribe to textbook definitions of management as a series of work elements composed of planning, organizing, directing, and controlling, or some similar group of discrete processes. (The connotation of *control* in this context is that of measuring progress against — or deviations from — plans and taking corrective action when and where needed.) There are very few managers who don't function along the lines of this model, but we have often detected a problem in the attention given to control and measurement. The emphasis in that important management process is heavily on financial controls, most of which provide their controlling function after the fact. Attempts to institute real-time control by computerization have been outstandingly successful in limited applications, but the thought of real-time control of overall business direction and results conjures up visions of managers buried under tons of computer output. Most of us are faced with the threat that if we take the measurement process seriously and make it a major part of our job, there will be little time left to do more creative things. Besides, the image of "mover and shaker" fits our self-concept in most instances better than that of the "controller."

MBO *requires* that a manager take the measurement process seriously and shift some emphasis into the monitoring of objectives and results. It also requires that this extra emphasis prevail at all levels in the organization.

The time required to do this properly must come from somewhere, and a poorly designed MBO system can indeed make such heavy demands that hard-working managers are quickly led to abandon the system. To avoid this cause of failure, the objectives that are to be monitored by managers other than the employee's immediate boss must be limited to the few that are of most importance to higher management. The guideline usually invoked suggests that 20 percent of the activities of an individual contribute 80 percent of his or her results. Therefore, objectives should be set and monitored only for that 20 percent. Such quasi-mathematical rules are hard to follow, but the suggestion is sound. Set a *few important* objectives and follow them *frequently* (continuously if necessary); monitor the other activities on the basis of *exception only.*[1]

Too frequent reviews lead to the feeling on the part of reviewer and reviewee that they have "been there before." If at successive reviews nothing substantial has changed and the participants feel

---

[1] The employee and the immediate manager are concerned, naturally, with *all* the objectives of the employee. Even between them, however, there must be some agreement about which ones to monitor formally (and at what intervals) and in which cases they should control "by exception" only.

that they are watching a soap opera, where it is possible to miss several episodes and still be fully informed, then the frequency of review should be changed.

On the other hand, the review of a project may result in a lively but inconclusive discussion, finally terminating in a mutual agreement by reviewer and reviewee that "we'd better move along and come back to this next time we meet." In these cases you should question whether the project is of sufficient importance to review at the present frequency (or at all). If decisions and corrective action on a project can be deferred continually with the consent of the boss, it must be a low-priority item.

Put such objectives to the "so what" test — ask what would happen if this objective were eliminated, left to the employee's self-measurement, reviewed less frequently, etc. Every effort must be made to keep the measurement process from becoming an end in itself rather than a means for eliminating obstacles, improving progress, and detecting the need for change. Overzealous or indiscriminate commitment to measurement can be as heavy a contributor to failure of MBO as undercommitment.

SURMOUNT-ING THE PROBLEM OF BUILT-IN PRIORITIES

Selection of the *wrong* objectives, even if they are achieved, is not likely to contribute to the desired overall results, except by chance. We must rely on you to recognize what is right for your organization and to evaluate the probabilities and uncertainties inherent in all decisions — and to live with the results. Only you can distinguish between the "must do" and the "nice to do," and there is little that we can do to help in that regard.

We do want to call your attention, though, to the problems created when responsibility for a project is taken on by an employee who already has a heavy continuing and unplanned workload. No matter how important the project work is in the eyes of the boss, the employee must continue to carry out the activities that contribute to the continuity of the business and to respond to the crises, queries, and complaints that regularly arise. The real demands of the business will dictate the person's distribution of time among the three job elements, and the priorities will adjust themselves accordingly, no matter what the a priori decision might have been. Invariably, the project work suffers, and again MBO has failed to live up to its promise.

The problem here is not in the recognition and selection of what is meaningful and important to the organization, but in the failure to acknowledge the strength of the built-in priorities that the continuing and unplanned activities exercise over project work. Project work is almost certain to be delayed beyond the target dates or otherwise fail to meet the objectives unless this inescapable fact is considered when the objectives are set.

One helpful technique is to require that a buffer of 20 percent or more of the employee's time remain uncommitted to allow for the inevitable changes in direction or crises. This will work only if either the employee or the boss (preferably both) has a good feel for how much time and personal effort is required to get project work done, and if unplanned job content does not increase significantly. The 20 percent buffer can quickly be swallowed up by underestimating either the magnitude of the project or the emergency work required.

Likewise, continuing responsibilities remove considerable discretion from the planning process. A sound estimate based on experience should be made of the time the employee can expect to spend on continuing operations, and this also should be subtracted from the time available for project activities. By limiting project commitments to match the discretionary time left after continuing and emergency needs are considered, you will substantially increase the probability of achieving project objectives. (We will explore this further in Unit 9 as part of the objective validation process.)

In all of this "hedging," as some will justifiably call it, one must recognize the temptation to conclude that "discretionary time simply doesn't exist in my job." The manager who hears this sad tale must *insist* that some time be set aside for improvement objectives of the type we have suggested in the two preceding units. Employees who feel this way must get off the treadmill long enough to catch their breath and examine the nature of their jobs and the available alternatives to the way they are operating. (A good first step in this direction would be to read Unit 3 of Vol. I and start the time-log analysis described in the exercises at the end of that unit.)

HOW DO YOU EAT AN ELEPHANT? BITE BY BITE!

Particularly in the early stages of MBO implementation, over-enthusiastic objective-setters often make the error of attempting to eat the elephant by swallowing it whole, that is, by stating a difficult objective in terms of its end point only, without breaking it down into manageable pieces. For example, consider the following objective:

> **❝** *We will achieve a 20 percent reduction in capping-machine downtime by year-end with a program that will entail not more than $1500 in cost per machine and will require not more than 6 man-weeks of engineering time to implement.* **❞**

The first question to ask is whether the "program" is fully thought out or whether its development is a part of the objective. Assuming that it does exist in well-developed form, the next question is "Has it been tried, and if not, will it work?" If the answers are not clearly "yes," this objective would be much less misleading and more assured of successful completion if it were broken up into (1) the development of a detailed design plan, (2) a trial on one or two machines, (3) modification as required, and (4) overall implementation. It might be, of course, that this is precisely the way the employee has approached it, but it is still advisable to *state* the intermediate milestones and completions, and to review progress at each point.

Let's suppose that after a trial in the machine development laboratory or in the plant (completed on schedule) it appears possible to meet or improve the downtime objective for $2000 per machine, instead of the $1500 target, with a total engineering expenditure of 12 man-weeks instead of the originally estimated 6. Measured against the objective as stated originally, this performance is wide of the mark. But if it were measured against an intermediate objective of determining the operating characteristics and the modification cost per machine, it would not only be a gauge of the performance of the individual but would also provide the basis for a decision to proceed with (or cancel) the project.

Eating the elephant bite by bite not only helps protect the employee from the risks of failure, but also provides much more guidance to both employee and boss in assessing progress, by giving early warning of the need to change direction and by indicating the need for joint decisions. Swallowing the whole elephant is surely a problem of inexperience, and the bite-by-bite approach is adopted intuitively by most seasoned employees. Managers who wish to adopt MBO, however, should be forewarned that if the objective-setting process is introduced too simplistically or in an authoritarian way, even your seasoned employees may feel pressured into setting "whole elephant" objectives which could have a high probability of failure.

OBJECTIVES AS A FORM OF PUNISHMENT

Employees often feel pressured. This feeling may be self-imposed, but too often it is the result of a punitive approach on the part of the manager. There is probably no surer way of inhibiting the improvement and innovation process (the reason MBO exists) than to create the feeling that failure to achieve an objective will result in censure by the boss, or in more subtle and lasting forms of punishment. Paradoxically, this leads to a very high rate of success in achieving individual objectives — your employees will make sure of that before they reveal them to you — but to an early demise of the MBO system as a whole. It will quickly be seen that MBO is not producing any improvements over the system it replaced.

Managing by objectives is a tempting notion to managers who have become frustrated by "human nature" or who interpret MBO to mean that they need not manage by *anything else* — that they needn't use judgment, know their people, or foster a helping relationship with them. To this group, MBO seems to offer an escape from the need to use judgment about people: "Either they meet their objectives or they don't." We will discuss this problem further in connection with the mutual objective-setting process in Unit 8. For now, we leave the subject with the warning that employees are prone to respond to this approach with games of their own, and that MBO based on such a shaky approach is doomed to failure.

ACTIVITY VERSUS RESULTS

Of all the many standards we listed in Unit 3 for measuring the quality and utility of an objective statement, ignoring the requirement of results orientation is probably the most dangerous to the health of an MBO system. Paradoxically again, this fault will not necessarily cause failure to achieve individual objectives. In fact, it may enhance their success, because in general it requires less creativity, skill, and effort to keep busy than it does to show results. But if objectives simply become the means of legitimizing activity which is in fact purposeless (or at least unmindful of the need for improvement) they contribute nothing to the success of the organization attempting to practice MBO.

Objectives expressed as activity can be a drain on profitability and can divert resources from desirable growth areas. Furthermore, because they seldom are directed at satisfying the needs of organizational claimants (if they were, they would in most cases be expressing desired results) such objectives allow the organization to focus on itself rather than on its mission—a certain forerunner of decay.

But, although the dangers are self-evident, it is not always easy to determine whether an objective is expressing results or activity. To illustrate, consider the well-known finding of the Surgeon General that cigarette smoking may be harmful to a person's health. Assume that, acting in accordance with its mission to transfer useful knowledge to the public, a unit of the Cooperative Extension Service, U. S. Department of Agriculture, sets an objective to conduct twelve short courses on "How to Stop Smoking" during the coming year. This is clearly activity-oriented if left in that form. If, however, the requirement is added that a minimum of one-third of all participants will give up smoking by the end of the course (or better yet, continue to abstain for 6 months after that), the results-orientation requirement is satisfied. And if indeed this result were obtained, we would conclude that the objective was achieved. So far, so good. However, in terms of the desired result—a decrease in the incidence of cancer among the participants in the program—the abstention from smoking is itself only an activity, and the results of this educational objective can finally be measured only after a number of years have passed.[2]

---

[2]It is instructive to follow this analysis to its logical conclusion. Obviously, the ultimate purpose is to lengthen human life. This purpose can be expressed in two ways which are quite different. The first is to lengthen the average life span of the population. The second is to reduce premature deaths from lung cancer among the heads of families with dependents. The latter might be seen as a more humanitarian purpose. But consider the fact that after a number of years of educational programs, publicity campaigns, and other measures since the Surgeon General's pronouncement, the number of smokers is on the increase. An analysis shows that the increase is among younger people who have many years of family responsibilities ahead of them. Feeding this new data back into the objective-setting process should result in a more effective focus on the nonsmoking educational effort, since it suggests that the target of such efforts should be teen-aged youth rather than the public in general. This illustrates the potential value of carrying the examination of purpose to its ultimate level. In this case, close examination proves helpful in establishing more specific short-term objectives, although not everyone would agree with the value judgments involved.

In spite of this conclusion, it would take an extreme defender of the primacy of results over activity to deny that the Extension education specialist who set the objectives had performed well. Activity and results have a very indistinct dividing line between them, and it is sometimes necessary to view any specific objective or its outcome in the total context to decide what the value of that outcome really is. If there is a well-established causal link between the achievement of an objective and the ultimate desired result, the achievement may be significant, even though the objective may involve only the completion of an activity. In Vol. III we suggest some more specific rules for appraising the effects of employee accomplishments that are not clearly results-oriented at first glance. Meanwhile, the best approach is to use caution when an objective appears activity-oriented and to probe for a cause-effect relationship between the activity and the desired result. The time to do this is during the joint objective-setting process. It is unfair to both manager and employee to ignore a potential problem of this magnitude until the employee's progress review or annual performance appraisal discussion.

COPING WITH THE "UNCONTROL- LABLES" We would like to predict dramatic results for MBO if all these pitfalls are avoided and if all our previous advice is heeded, but we will not yield to that temptation. There are too many uncontrollable factors affecting the degree of success in an organization to claim that *any* system of management will guarantee success. Many failures of MBO to demonstrate visibly improved results over some earlier period are caused by a combination of unfavorable competitive or environmental conditions and a measurement system that is not sophisticated enough to isolate the effects of the major variables.

Unless the fluctuation in profitability from one period to the next can be broken down into the effects of sales volume, price, product mix, labor and material variances, and other factors, favorable effects resulting from objectives set and met are difficult to claim. Breakdowns are needed, even within any one of these factors. For example, the effects of successfully closing several major targeted sales accounts can be completely masked by a general overall downturn in business.

When a management group commits itself to the demands of MBO, it must also decide to accept the burden of developing more sophisticated measurements of organizational success. Without these measurements, it runs the risk of abandoning a management system that may in fact be producing excellent but unidentifiable results. The opposite may also be true; MBO undertaken in an economic upturn may get credit for a degree of success for which it is not responsible. This makes it doubly disillusioning when it "fails" to sustain that level of results in the next downturn.

The continual monitoring of progress that takes place under MBO enables managers to anticipate, or at least receive early warning of, changes in the environment and to maintain the organization in a more adaptive mode. Therefore, we can confidently say that MBO puts a small measure of control on the uncontrollables, but it can never eliminate them or their effects.

We won't subject you to an exercise covering this unit. You have had or will have opportunities to practice avoiding most of these pitfalls and problems elsewhere in this series. Go on to Unit 7, where we discuss some special situations in objective setting.

UNIT 7

SPECIAL CASES IN OBJECTIVE SETTING

The "doers" in an organization should find little difficulty in formulating objectives for themselves if they follow the suggestions made in the preceding units. Those who have primarily leadership or advisory responsibilities, however, or those who are in a largely staff advisory role, may need to spend time considering what kinds of objectives are appropriate for expressing their potential contributions. We have in mind persons in the managerial and staff functions of an organization. Staff functions are held by most writers to be the most difficult areas into which to introduce MBO. While managers are more directly responsible for identifiable "results," they still must ask to what extent their objectives are merely the summation of those of their subordinates, and to what extent these objectives should be different, or unique to the management function.

In this unit we will deal with these issues. They concern not only the selection of objectives but also the establishment of measures of performance in areas often regarded as unmeasurable—measures that must depend heavily on judgment and, in some cases, on anticipating effects far in the future. For example, how does one establish objectives for, or measure the contribution of, the head of the legal department whose main job is to steer the firm through the shoals of antitrust law? Are the results determinable only in cases where his or her advice is bad? And what share of the total contribution, however it is measured, comes from the achievements of the subordinates in the department and how much from the manager? When we begin to ponder such questions, we quickly see the real limitations of "hard" measurements in situations like these. It also becomes easy to understand why MBO is often resisted by staff people and accepted by managers only as it applies to their subordinates.

We offer no quick or simple solution to implementation problems like these. But we trust that the thoughts expressed in this unit will make the objective-setting process more meaningful and acceptable to those of you who are in, or responsible for, staff, managerial, or other hard-to-measure activities.

THE MANAGER'S OBJECTIVES

It is tempting for the manager of a component to consider his or her objectives simply as the totality of those of the subordinates. In the terminology of the means-ends chain (see Unit 4), the manager may adopt the ends (objective statements) developed in support of the next higher level objectives as his or her own or, even less specifically, may fall back on the means statement itself. For example, the design section manager in Fig. 4 might make redesigning the spot-welder a personal objective. The fallacy is easy to see; the manager is, in effect, riding on the coattails of all the subordinates whose activities and objectives support him or her.

Even less productively, the manager might be tempted to use means statements, represented in Fig. 4 as "Implement downtime study recommendations with needed equipment design changes," as personal objectives. Managers who do this add the sins of vagueness and generality to the one already mentioned.

It is conceivable, especially in smaller organizations or in lower levels of management, that the manager may indeed develop personal objectives in the technical area for which he or she retains action responsibility and accountability. These objectives are, of course, perfectly legitimate as long as the manager does not develop a tendency to "hang onto things," which persists even when the demands of the true management functions (planning, organizing, controlling, etc.) increase with growing leadership and administrative responsibilities. The true management functions provide ample opportunities for personal objective setting for most managers without an additional involvement in technical work, especially when the job consists of managing other managers.

Some likely sources for managerial objectives are needs for improvement or change in these areas:

The image of the component or the company, with top management, customers, or the public

Removal of obstacles to smooth the flow of work and information

Review and revision of strategic plans

Review of planning procedures, organization structure, compensation plan, etc.

Personal involvement in negotiations, acquisitions, reorganizations, financing efforts, etc.

Employee development

Personal study and improvement (e.g., learn conversational Japanese, study information theory, etc.)

The last two, employee and self-development, are common to all management jobs and deserve further attention. The need for self-development exists, of course, in all jobs, nonmanagerial as well as managerial. Our special emphasis on it is based on the tendency of many managers to overlook the need to continue developing their capabilities in the management profession. (This need for continuing professional development is recognized to a much greater extent by those in other professions and in technical specialties.)

The need for employee development takes many forms:

Development of selected employees to meet the organization's needs

Improved procedures for performance measurement, review, and correction

Promoting joint problem-solving activities with the concerned subordinates

Improved skills in delegation to promote employee growth and effectiveness

Several examples of objective/plan statements in the employee and self-development areas are shown in Table 4. This table introduces an objective form not mentioned previously that has considerable value in individual development—*self-commitment*. This is a private statement of intent, usually shared with no one else, that

Table 4
Selection of Objectives for Managers, Based on Employee and Self-Development Needs

Activity Type	Typical Needs for Improvement	Appropriate Ways to Express an Objective	Examples of Objective/Plan Statements
Employee Development	Prepare subordinate for assuming manager's duties during latter's extended leave	Approval criterion with problem-solving program	1. Get approval of plan by higher management by departure day (D) minus 6 months. Plan to include the following steps, to be implemented on schedule indicated: a. Determine how to inform other subordinates and make this part of plan for higher manager's approval. b. Inform subordinate of plan immediately upon approval. c. Send subordinate to Supervisory Development Institute. D minus 5 months. d. Assign subordinate to executive committee as my replacement. D minus 4 months e. Schedule weekly coaching sessions starting D minus 4 months.
	Implement MBO effectively with subordinates	Implicit standard of performance (frequency of review) with backup program to implement	1. Attend Face-to-Face Performance Appraisal Techniques Seminar, Baltimore, September 6–8. 2. Schedule and implement the following continuing program of quarterly work-planning and review sessions: a. Initial objective setting with all six subordinates individually, week ending 10/6 (fiscal week 13). b. Repeat reviews during fiscal weeks 26, 39, and 52. 3. Inform all subordinates of this proposed schedule by 9/15 in staff meeting discussion. 4. Incorporate their suggestions on timing and format prior to first objective-setting session.
Self-Development	Change in future job requirements	Self-commitment	1. Call university extension today and obtain information on underwriting courses offered. 2. Enroll in one 3-hour night course in spring semester starting 2/11.

relies on internal motivation as its driving force. The motivation is reinforced by putting the statement into writing as a firm commitment to oneself. (It should be obvious that the act of writing it down has no motivational value per se without *a prior decision based on a felt need*. Once that decision is made, however, the "formal contract" with oneself can help sustain the degree of commitment.)

Each managerial employee should be required to establish improvement objectives in the realm of professional management work — planning, organizing, staffing, controlling, or whatever your "model" of the management job includes as components. No one in the organization can afford to assume that opportunities in these areas do not exist. Neither can any manager rest secure in objectives that are really those of his or her subordinates. If a manager cannot find any others, there are only two possible answers: a state of perfection exists, or the position or its incumbent is not really an asset to the organization. The former is unlikely, but the latter situation has been known to exist. In any event, testing a manager's ability to formulate personal objectives can be very revealing to the boss.

STAFF OBJECTIVES

Members of organizational components whose main function is to provide services to the line (production) components may feel they are out of the mainstream and may find it difficult to accept the idea of stating results-oriented objectives for themselves. Their posture of readiness to serve imposed by the unpredictable demands of their internal clients creates a natural defensiveness when the subject of measurement arises. This is especially the case when the service offered is in the highly intangible form of advice and counsel as opposed to the fairly "hard" output of, for example, the purchasing section or the company cafeteria. Measurement of the latter services in terms of cost savings, employee reaction, and other results is more or less readily accepted by their members. But how can we persuade the legal advisor to set or accept goals and objectives for self or for the functional group? The output here is professional advice, and as a professional, he or she cannot and will not admit to providing anything less than the best, which leaves little room for thinking of improvement objectives. We have picked an extreme case to emphasize that a quite different approach needs to be cultivated in introducing MBO to some staff functions.

We find the most useful approach to staff objective setting is through the notion of the functional KRA discussed in Unit 4. Sometimes after a staff manager or specialist has translated organizational KRAs into functional KRAs to which the staff component can contribute, it becomes more apparent what types of objectives are called for.

Another method, distasteful but often effective in stimulating thought, is to require an answer to the question, "What if this staff component did not exist, or were eliminated?" This is the underlying question in zero-base budgeting, of course. Asked in this context, it forces a hard look at staff results, which can then be used as the basis for determining improvement needs.

Either of these two approaches can be effective in broadening the staff employee's thinking in terms of results. The second is likely to be construed as threatening when and if posed by the boss, and should be used with care. It is less threatening if zero-base budgeting is in effect and has been assimilated into the organization's culture, but under those conditions the problem of staff objectives has probably already been surmounted.

Even though it is not easy to measure the results of staff services, the improvement of their level and quality should be considered the subject of objectives for the function. The staff manager or specialist should consider such goals as:

Increased accessibility of staff functions to line personnel

Increased responsiveness, timeliness, and improved staff-line relationships

Effectiveness and timeliness of transfer of new techniques to line operations

Improved cost effectiveness of services with respect to available alternate (external) services

Opportunities for cost savings resulting from operation audits and studies

STANDARDS OF STAFF PERFORMANCE At the root of the difficulty and resistance encountered in setting staff objectives is the widespread lack of performance standards for staff functions. Line operations have become accustomed to standard times, standard costs, and other targets that represent a continuing challenge to improvement. "To meet 19__ standards" is a perfectly valid expression of the major objective of most production components (when those standards have been spelled out clearly and the objectives backed up with a plan). But for staff operations in general, the issue of standards has seldom been addressed.

There are many bases for establishing standards of performance or levels of excellence that the staff function (or any other function considering the establishment of standards for the first time) might adopt. As shown in Fig. 5, these may involve comparisons with external competition, with internal performances that can serve as models, with theoretical or ideal performances, or even with your own present performance. Finally, lacking any other suitable basis, a reasonable and mutually acceptable challenge by the boss or a proposal by the employee can serve as a starting point.

A glance down the list in Fig. 5 will show a general decrease in toughness and objectivity from top to bottom. However, any of these bases is useful and valid in making a start. One obvious axiom of objective setting is that it makes little sense to state where you are going if you don't know where you are now. Even the least preferred judgmental standard involves some acknowledgement of where you are now and an admission that it is not where you want to be.

---

1. *Best that the competition does*
    e.g., Industry or association statistics, National Safety Council, patents issued

2. *Best that you have ever done*
    e.g., Your best year ever
        Average of your three best *recent* years
        Your best department or unit

3. *Theoretical figure*
    e.g., Zero defects, error-free performance, ideal CPM schedule

4. *No worse than you are now*
    The *trend* is what counts — up is good, down is bad

5. *An acceptable challenge*
    e.g., By your boss: "Let's see if you can improve your manpower efficiency by 10 percent in the next two years."

6. *Pure judgment*
    i.e., "This is what I think should be acceptable" or "This is what I think others will view as acceptable." (backed up by defensible reasons)

FIGURE 5
Bases for establishing standards of performance

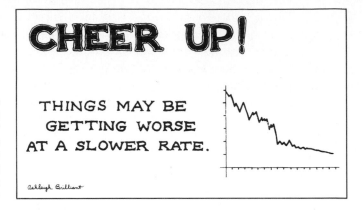

The comparison with competition is probably the most useful approach. It has a major role in the strategic planning process (see Vol. I) for the overall organization, and should be a major input in functional staff strategy as well. Information is available from a wide range of sources for any area of staff endeavor—the average industry wage settlements in union contract negotiations, the number of patents assigned to competitors, evidence of the cash-management practices of competition (many other clues to competitive financial management are available from financial statements), readership ratings, etc.[1]

THE INESCAPABLE ROLE OF JUDGMENT

In Unit 3 we stressed the requirement that objectives be measurable. In the case of staff objectives, this is especially difficult to achieve. The results of staff studies and recommendations are often not known for months or even years. (This delay also negates the value of feedback of the results in improving current operations, one of the chief benefits of MBO performance appraisal and review.) Furthermore, the contributory nature of staff work makes it doubly difficult to isolate and measure the value of that work in relation to the total effort.

---

[1]Merely attempting to ape the competition, however, is not necessarily conducive to the best use of the organization's resources. Before you accept a competitor's performance in any respect as your own objective, we suggest you review the material on competitive analysis in Vol. I.

These difficulties do not reflect inadequacies in the MBO concept, but are simply reminders that *no system of management* can or should obviate the need for *managerial judgment* in the assessment of performance or in the selection of objectives for the organization or the individual.

It is judgment that is called into play when we ask "What would happen if this function or activity were eliminated?" When we call the simple *completion* of an activity or project an achieved objective, judgment is again used because of the belief that a direct cause-effect relationship exists between the activity and the desired end result. And, although attempts to measure the results of management development and of continuing education are often frustrating (indeed, such efforts are called an "act of faith" by some authorities) it is judgment that prevails in the decision to use this approach to human resource development.

The effort to establish objectives in the difficult-to-measure areas of a business does not always lead to quantitative answers. But at least it raises pertinent questions about actual and potential performance. In so doing, this effort attempts to substitute measurement for pure judgment, if such an opportunity exists. Failing in this, it highlights the need to make reasoned judgments.

For example, suppose that the boss sits down with his or her legal counsel to develop measurable objectives for the position. They might first try to establish a quantitative basis for measurement, such as the number of cases won, or the dollar savings in reduced judgments against the firm that the counsel has obtained. The discussion would, we hope, quickly lead to the conclusion that the counsel should concentrate major effort on the *preventive* aspects of the job—ideally, the "best" number in both these proposed measurements is zero. This could be realized only if the counsel, with legal advice, succeeded completely in keeping the firm out of trouble, and then only if he or she were able to influence almost every action the firm takes affecting the public. The discourse might then turn to the selection of major areas of concern—e.g., consumer action, environmental protection, antitrust action—and finally to the development of objectives. Achievement of these objectives would reflect the combined judgment of the counsel and the manager that an excellent effort is being carried out in the chosen areas. The objectives might include a long-range decline in the number and severity of formal actions taken by regulatory agencies or, on a short-term basis, the strengthening of the counsel's educational efforts with operating managers.

Whatever the resulting objectives may be, the search for staff objectives is certain to lead to a more effective exercise of managerial direction and control than if no attempt at measurement were made. In any case, managers cannot afford to exclude staff functions from their MBO programs simply because of staff resistance or the difficulties of measurement.

THE DO-OR-DIE OBJECTIVE

Frequently a natural disaster, a competitive coup, or an internal malfunction will place an organization in jeopardy, giving rise to a managerial edict that violates both the principle of joint objective setting and the rule that an objective must have a backup plan before it is mutually acceptable. Under conditions of severe stress, the rules of conventional MBO must, of course, be temporarily set aside. The acceptance of an objective by edict can often be the opportunity for the employee to prove his or her capability in a manner that years of conventional experience may not provide. The reputation of capable troubleshooter has been the ticket to advancement for many who responded effectively to a do-or-die objective.

Do-or-die objectives can be expressed in the following terms:

"Pumping Station 8 must be back on line by September 1."

"I'll give you 6 months to turn that operation around and put it in the black."

"We must be ready by November 1 with a gasoline rationing plan that can be put into effect in 60 days."

Such objectives leave little doubt about *what* has to be done, or about its importance (at least as seen by the boss). The question becomes one of *how* they are to be accomplished, or the establishment of a type 2 objective or action plan. We will briefly cover the necessary skills and methods in the final unit of this volume. These are largely the techniques of the field known as *project management*, which has proved effective in meeting such seemingly impossible challenges as the one laid down by President Kennedy in 1960 — to have Americans on the moon within the decade.

Before accepting such a do-or-die objective, the employee is entitled to know from the manager:

The precise criteria of successful accomplishment (the project scope and specifications)

The tasks or responsibilities that can be allocated elsewhere, dropped, or deferred

The resources available to accomplish the task — financial, human, and physical — and the limits of the authority delegated to the employee

It is apparent, then, that the joint objective-setting session is still important to the employee in resolving many potential problems and in clarifying the task, despite the fact that the objective itself has been imposed autocratically.

OBJECTIVES AT THE OPERATIVE LEVEL

Relatively few organizations have extended MBO procedures to all levels, including the individual worker in the shop or on the factory floor. Often hampered in their thinking by restrictive union contracts or by perceived mistrust between union leaders and managers, most managers feel that MBO should be confined to the salaried ranks. Although there is a trend toward performance appraisal procedures that reflect concrete performance rather than generalized personality traits, few first-line managers are ready to embrace the idea of joint objective setting (with the loss of management control that it connotes) whether or not there is a collective bargaining unit present. Other managers feel limited by wage administration policies that make it difficult to reward hourly rated employees for improved performance. Still others believe that hourly rated jobs are so structured as to leave little opportunity for the worker to play any meaningful role in objective setting.

In spite of all this, there are a few firms which have introduced objective setting at all levels, including that of the hourly worker, with considerable success. One of the better-known examples is Texas Instruments, Inc. TI has found that a comprehensive program of worker involvement is a prerequisite to successful objective setting at the lower levels. Team formation at the worker level, reduction or elimination of many status differences between workers and supervisors, and a management group that *listens* to employees are some of the significant features of the TI approach to worker involvement. Mark Shepard, Jr., chief executive officer, states, "We've found that if you get people involved, they'll set tougher goals for themselves than you would dare do. And have fun doing it."[2]

A word of caution is necessary, however. True successes, those lasting over a period of years, have invariably been preceded—as at Texas Instruments—by management's full and wholehearted acceptance of the humanistic principles covered in the next unit (and in Vol. III), and by an almost missionary zeal in applying the principles to the whole work force. Before you seriously consider applying MBO at the worker level, be sure that it is working well and has been accepted by all levels of management, not only as a rational structure for carrying on the management process, but also as a means of fostering employee growth, dignity, and involvement in management. It is especially important to have the support of first-line supervisors. People who have reached that hard-won position may at first regard joint objective setting with their workers as a threat to their authority. Since first-line supervisors are the only representatives of management with whom most workers ever come in contact, this important group must understand and accept the principles involved to convey to the workers the true purpose and meaning of the MBO approach.

Of all the objections cited to worker-level MBO, the most rational is the hesitancy to apply objective setting to jobs that are completely structured. Unless a job allows a moderate degree of worker discretion in such decisions as how to do the job, in what order to carry out the work elements, or how to monitor quality, objectives are severely limited. This limitation does not obviate the need for feedback to the worker about the need for perfect attendance, error-free performance, and similar goals. However, objectives that tap worker creativity and other higher-level motivations require elbow room on the job—freedom to try out new approaches, ideas, and methods. Objective setting is much more likely to be (and has been) successful when dealing with an office

---

[2]For an excellent treatment of the overall subject of worker participation, written by the founder of the Texas Instruments program, see M. Scott Myers, *Every Employee a Manager* (New York: McGraw-Hill, 1970).

custodial force or a city government's refuse collection crew than with the workers on an auto assembly line.

Most organizations that have successfully applied joint objective setting to highly structured jobs have found it necessary to first redesign the jobs, allowing workers to play a major role. Typically, a series of assembly line operations are restructured so that a team performs all the work elements, having considerable latitude as to which worker carries out a specific operation. Rotation is allowed, work assignments are made by the group, and peripheral tasks such as inspection are added to the total scope of work. In some cases direct supervision is eliminated, with managers available only as needed to provide assistance and feedback and for joint negotiation of objectives with the group. Volvo, the Swedish auto maker, is an example of this system in action.

The Volvo program is based on the elimination of auto assembly line worker specialization. The approach is to put the assembly of the whole auto in the hands of teams of workers. Within the teams each worker can rotate among jobs, advance to the limits of his or her capability, and exercise a role in the leadership of the team. Although minimum production standards for each model are set at the plant level, and the production process is dictated to a large extent by quality requirements, there is considerable latitude for short-range objective setting by the team. Work team members are also included in higher-level team activities such as new designs or production process changes, where they also contribute to objective setting and action planning. The extent of Volvo's management commitment to the program is reflected in the heavy expenditures for basic production layout changes necessitated by the redesigned work setup.

Objectives at the worker level may be set individually, but usually they are set on a team basis, even when job redesign is not required. The basis may be the three-man crew operating and loading a garbage compactor, the four custodians assigned to the branch bank, or the twelve chemical plant operators running the nitration process. Group identification and feelings of mutual support add to the dignity and satisfaction of the work, and the opportunities for group discussion build upon the creativeness of each individual. There is potential for a higher level of worker motivation, quality consciousness, and other favorable results. However, we advise that you survey the experiences of others who have followed this path before you decide to implement worker-level MBO, and we repeat our warning that you must have the system well consolidated at the management level before you even consider extending it further.

In the next unit we will discuss the important part that joint objective setting plays in adding the humanistic dimension to the logical, rational framework of MBO.

EXERCISE 7

1. From your viewpoint as an employee, list several objectives you would like to see your boss accept as his or her own. Indicate the desired effect of each on your own work objectives, professional and personal.

Boss's Objective	Desired Effect on My Work Objectives

2. Here is a list of staff position titles. For those with which you are familiar, (a) propose a potential area for improvement which the incumbent might use to formulate one or more objectives; (b) add positions of concern to you in your own organization and do the same.

Position	Improvement Opportunity
Advertising manager	
Chief auditor	
Cost accounting manager	

Position	Improvement Opportunity
Food services manager	
Legal counsel	
Management development coordinator	
Marketing research manager	
Medical services director	
Planning and zoning administrator	
Public relations director	

Position	**Improvement Opportunity**
Purchasing director	
Quality assurance manager	
Research director	
Chief safety engineer	
Tax assessor	
Union relations manager	
Others:	

Commentary on Exercise 7

1. We put you in the employee's position to focus your attention on managerial objectives designed to remove obstacles, enhance productivity of subordinates, and provide for management and professional development. You might have wanted your boss to include such objectives as:

> Increase frequency of feedback to employees on perceptions of their performance
>
> Allocate funds for formal education and training of selected subordinates
>
> Revise a policy that is having a negative effect on employee performance
>
> Reach an agreement with a fellow manager on division of responsibilities in an area causing intergroup friction
>
> Provide tools or facilities designed to improve employee productivity

Now place yourself in your own present or future position as manager and translate *your* employees' needs into objectives for yourself. Some of these may take the form of self-commitments.

2. Your examples of improvement opportunities might have included the following:

Advertising manager	Increase cost effectiveness of space advertising
Chief auditor	Add management audit competence to staff
Cost accounting manager	Determine needs for cost analyses not now provided
Food services manager	Increase percentage of employee patronage by offering box lunch option
Legal counsel	Institute periodic bulletin to management on pending legislation, pertinent rulings, etc.
Management development coordinator	Develop plan for regional assessment center
Marketing research manager	Develop series of leading indicators specific to the business
Medical services director	Develop in-house capability for executive physical examinations

Planning and zoning administrator	Draw up minimum specifications for energy loss and consumption in single-family dwellings
Public relations director	Establish speakers' bureau for company executives
Purchasing director	Develop third sources for all class A purchased items
Quality assurance manager	Establish vendor certification program to reduce incoming material inspection costs
Research director	Complete study of critical path of the product development process to reduce lead time to production
Chief safety engineer	Establish hazard analysis procedure in all plants to reduce process and product risks
Tax assessor	Prepare proposal for annual reassessment to council
Union relations manager	Prepare workshop on grievance avoidance, based on analysis of most frequent claims of contract violation

If you are an experienced staff person in any of the above positions, the chances are that you are already availing yourself of the opportunity we have suggested. It's up to you to take it from there and explore the job potential as only *you* can.

If you are managing staff who have never been required to set improvement goals, we hope this exercise has given you some ideas on the types of improvement to explore jointly with them.

UNIT 8

THE JOINT OBJECTIVE-SETTING PROCESS

The whole MBO system depends heavily on the successful execution of two key events, the objective-setting conference and the performance review. Both of these are one-to-one dialogues between manager and employee. They require certain skills — listening, interviewing, negotiating on a face-to-face basis, resolving conflict without sweeping it under the rug, and delegation, to name a few. We will deal only briefly with the development of these skills.[1] Many good sources cover these topics in depth, and it would far exceed the scope of this series to attempt to treat adequately the whole field of interpersonal communication.

---

[1] We have deferred much of this coverage, particularly interviewing and delegation skills, to Vol. III, where they are treated as aspects of performance review. Performance review tends to be a more difficult and emotionally charged experience for most managers and employees than objective setting, and as a result depends more heavily on these interpersonal skills for its success.

However, prerequisite to your acceptance of the need to *acquire* skill in these areas, is an understanding of the purpose of and the potential for doing these things well. Much of the benefit of your MBO program depends on your understanding and acceptance of the ideas of *power equalization* and of *harmony between individual and organizational needs.* Your intelligent application of these ideas to your organization can mean the difference between merely turning your organization *around* with MBO and turning it *on.*

INDIVIDUAL NEEDS VERSUS ORGANIZATIONAL DEMANDS

The individual and the organization are often in an unnecessary state of conflict because of disharmony between individual and organizational needs (which the employee often interprets as demands). The two should exist in a mutually supportive relationship: one in which both the individual and the organization are stimulated to growth and nurtured by the relationship.

In some respects this mutual support is self-evident. The employee provides services that the firm needs for its growth in exchange for immediate and deferred compensation and benefits that provide subsistence, discretionary income, and a measure of security. In most organizations the employee can also satisfy (at least partly) needs for social interaction and acceptance by a peer group. These employee needs fall into the categories proposed by the psychologist Abraham Maslow,[2] referred to as *lower-level* or *deficiency* needs. Maslow theorized that all human needs show a hierarchical pattern in which the lower levels command the attention of the person until each is filled or partially satisfied, at which point the next higher level exerts dominance and the person becomes concerned with seeking ways of satisfying that level. In order of ascendancy, the five categories are subsistence needs (physiological needs, such as food and water), safety and security needs, social needs (belonging), ego or identity needs, and self-actualization needs. The last of these is most simply described as the need to become the best that one is capable of becoming — to use all one's skills and talents to experience the ultimate growth and maturity that the human organism can achieve.

---

[2]Abraham Maslow, *Motivation and Personality* (New York: Harper & Row, 1954).

Modern organizations are frequently accused of providing the opportunities for satisfaction of only the first three of these levels. By failing to arouse and satisfy the higher-level (identity and self-actualization) needs in employees, most organizations unknowingly and perhaps in some rare cases, deliberately) hold individuals in a state of immaturity or incomplete psychological development, thereby denying them the opportunity for full growth and fulfillment. At the same time, of course, the organization does not receive the maximum contribution from its work force.

The ego/identity needs are those based on achievement and recognition. These are satisfied in the work setting by opportunities for exercising self-control, autonomy, participation as a respected member of the organization, advancement, increase in responsibility, freedom to exercise creativity and discretion, and through other evidence of the dignity and importance of the employee. The research of behavioral scientist Frederick Herzberg[3] has revealed that the positive motivation of a wide range of workers, from menial to managerial, depends heavily on the satisfaction of higher-level needs. On the other hand, problems affecting lower-level needs tend to be demotivators if not handled well and, at best, provide little positive motivation.

The well-known Theory Y of Douglas MacGregor assumes that work is a natural outlet for human desires, among them the desire to exercise self-control, to seek responsibility in the support of worth-while objectives, to create, and to grow. MacGregor predicted that managers who make such assumptions will behave toward their subordinates in a way that will result in greater organizational effectiveness than can be obtained by managers who make a generally opposite set of assumptions. MacGregor called this Theory X.[4] Theory X managers, according to MacGregor, assume that work is something that most people want to avoid, that people will not exercise self-control or responsibility willingly, and that they require close supervision and narrowly defined jobs. In effect, MacGregor was describing a Theory Y manager as one who assumes that all human beings are driven primarily by Maslow's higher-level needs, while a Theory X manager assumes that lower-level needs are uppermost in the work force.

---

[3]Frederick Herzberg, *Work and the Nature of Man* (New York: World, 1966).
[4]Douglas MacGregor, *The Human Side of Enterprise* (New York: McGraw-Hill, 1960).

Maslow, Herzberg, and MacGregor have expressed what is clearly a single, unified concept, and a number of organizations, public and private, have been sufficiently impressed by the logic of this concept to make basic changes in their approach to employees. The results of such attempts to tap the unutilized potential of human resources have been mixed. Appealing to the higher-lever human needs has in some cases produced dramatic results, but it has become apparent that this approach cannot be used universally. The work force is too diverse in the patterns of needs that characterize its individual members. Success does not seem to depend on the class of work or the level of worker involved. It can be as wrong to assume that *every* professional employee will respond to Theory Y management (or to higher-level need satisfiers) as it is to assume that *every* laborer responds only to the lower-level needs for order, structure, predictability, and security.

The tremendous range of individual backgrounds and experiences and the resulting variations within any group of employees call for a highly individualized approach to leadership. Other situational variations from group to group and task to task (and even within the same group or task, as economic and other outside influences vary) also require a highly adaptive approach to management.

Management by objectives provides the framework in which this range of management styles can be carried out. The nature of the one-to-one relationship between manager and employee is readily adaptable not just to the needs and capabilities of the individual employee but also to the situation in which the organization or component finds itself at that time.[5] In the preceding unit we defended the legitimacy of the do-or-die objective as an opportunity for the employee and as an expression of the organization's right and duty to demand performance when it is threatened. In this unit we will examine the other side of the coin — the joint objective-setting process, its effect on the satisfaction of higher-level employee needs, and its potential for meeting the organization's needs.

---

[5] The prevalent belief of many proponents of a particular management style is that any variation from that style is upsetting and confusing to subordinates, and that the manager's credibility suffers as a result. We give most employees credit for perceiving the situation accurately. We are firmly convinced that they *expect* a manager to behave differently as the situation changes, and that they would be more distressed to see the manager behaving "consistently" when that consistency fails to reflect reality as they know it.

MBO AND HIGHER-LEVEL HUMAN NEEDS

Because of its structure, the MBO system has the potential for satisfying higher-level human needs even without the face-to-face interaction provided in the objective-setting and performance review phases. The well-run organization fosters achievement and self-actualization on the part of its employees, even without MBO. It does this by designing jobs to include significant breadth of activity and responsibility, and by carefully selecting incumbents on the basis of skills and interests that encourage them to function fully within the scope of the job. The structural features of MBO—the hierarchy of objectives, the means-ends chain, and the emphasis on individual contributions to important company programs—add to the individual's sense of identity. This structure emphasizes the role of individuals in the pursuit of organizational excellence by clearly relating their efforts to the larger task.

On the surface, it would seem that an organization can satisfy many higher-level employee needs without the close manager-employee relationship that is required to implement our MBO system to the fullest extent. This is especially true when the organization is in a dynamic growth phase, providing ample opportunities for capable people to advance.

So it is not surprising that many successful managers bridle at the behavioral scientists' allegation that their organizations are repressing the psychological growth of their employees. The evidence of growth surrounds them on every side, in the form of employees who are happily doing what they like to do and receiving recognition in the form of advancement, increased responsibility, and respect from clients, customers, and peers. They may also be experiencing the challenge and thrill of achieving important objectives.

THE PSYCHOLOGICAL ENVIRONMENT

The preceding analysis fails to recognize the important role that the immediate manager (the boss) plays in shaping the psychological environment in which the employee functions. True, job scope, peer relationships, organizational structure and policies also make up a large part of that environment, but the boss is probably the largest single influence. For example, he or she is the immediate connecting link in the communication chain, transmitting organizational purpose, priorities, and feedback to the employee. If that link is missing or weak, or if communication is often distorted or presented in a dictatorial, uncaring, or capricious way, much of the real environment may be affected in an adverse way. If feedback on performance (covered extensively in Vol. III) is neglected, distorted, or manipulated to meet the boss's needs rather than the employee's, the environment is again polluted. Finally, through careless or inequitable interpretation and application of organizational policy and procedures, the boss can often convey to the employee a picture of the environment that is quite different from the way it was designed.

POWER REDISTRIBUTION AND THE HELPING RELATIONSHIP

Managers' actions such as those discussed above are by no means always deliberate. In most cases they are probably not even recognized by the boss as being part of his or her behavior pattern. But, deliberate or unconscious, most of us are guilty of such actions to some extent. For example, a frequent reaction of employees, when first approached with the need to set improvement objectives, is one of anxiety or fear. The emotions underlying these expressions include mistrust of the boss's intentions, fear of his or her power, and feelings of personal inadequacy or inferiority. We are not speaking about isolated instances, but of employee concerns so prevalent that they can only be explained by a history of boss-employee relations in which *the boss's behavior* has played a major part in creating these feelings.

The boss may not be reflecting his or her real nature in acting this way. If top-level managers "model" this behavior for their employees, each manager at a successively lower level may in turn set the same example, regardless of the natural inclinations he or she may have toward others. In some organizations, to be a winner, a young manager *must* conform to the model set by a single top-level person — and by those who are striving to be like him.

To overcome these negative feelings about the boss in general and objective setting in particular, all managers need to be constantly aware of their power and of their major role in the psychological environment. "Power" has become a much maligned concept, primarily because of its misuse by those in positions of authority. In fact, however, power is a necessary factor in *any* human relationship. It is defined simply as the ability to influence others, and carries no inherent connotations of evil. The problem stems from the manner in which it is exercised and from the underlying motives. The power exerted by organizational leaders can have the highest motives (the fulfillment of all its members' societal needs), or the lowest (the leaders' personal enrichment or aggrandizement). But even when the motives are of the highest, the manner in which power is exercised can be demeaning to the subordinate, destroying self-confidence, denying his or her adulthood, and generally creating the dependency, mistrust, suspicion, and fear we find so widespread. When the motive ascribed to management for introducing MBO is "to hold our feet to the fire" (as is so often the case), managers must examine their leadership practices, to salvage not only their MBO program but also the human assets of the enterprise.

Two statements (the first representing the problem and the second the solution) will serve to bring all this philosophizing down to cases. The first, by a teacher in the Wisconsin public schools, typifies the negative reactions to MBO in the field of education, a field that ranks high among those that could benefit from an MBO orientation:

Drawing by
Joseph Farris; © 1977
The New Yorker
Magazine, Inc.

"If I may say so, and I certainly may say so . . ."

> ❝ *Conceived in deceit and born in arrogance . . . the concept of MBO . . . will prove to be one of the most counter-productive forces in the field of education . . . . As a concept lending itself to so-called accountability, it serves no master other than the individual who envisions it as providing him with . . . a bludgeon . . .*[6] ❞

This is a strong statement, but it typifies a large sector of employee opinion in all kinds of organizations. We must take it seriously and ask whether it is the result of long experience with authority figures who have used their power and status excessively or carelessly.

The second statement describes a redistribution of management power as practiced by a large food distributor (Jewel Companies, Inc.) and demonstrates the helping relationship that exists between that firm's managers and their subordinates:

> ❝ *. . . each management person thinks of himself not as the order-giving, domineering boss, but as the first assistant to those who 'report' to him in a more typical organizational sense. Thus we mentally turn our organization charts upside down and challenge ourselves to seek ways in which we can lead—by helping—by teaching—by listening—and by managing in the true democratic sense—that is, with the consent of the managed. Thus the satisfactions of leadership come from helping others to get things done—not from getting credit for doing and changing things ourselves.*[7] ❞

The concept of *power redistribution* was first introduced by psychologist Harold Leavitt in 1962. Leavitt used a stronger term, *power equalization,* defining it as the reduction in the power and status differential between supervisors and subordinates. The statement from Jewel Companies is an excellent definition of the concept in terms of managerial behavior. At the same time, the statement

---

[6]Richard Brown, "The Truth About MBO," *Wisconsin Journal of Education,* September 1972, p. 12.

[7]Donald S. Perkins, Chairman and chief executive officer of Jewel Companies, Inc., *Progressive Grocer,* September 1973, p. 76.

may raise questions in many readers' minds as to how much power can be redistributed without destroying the organization, and indeed how seriously the statement is regarded by lower-level employees.

Certainly, many important aspects of power must be retained by management in any organization. We will return to some of these aspects in the next section of this unit. But it is important to realize that the status differential between manager and subordinate—even if the manager does not consciously exert an effort to maintain that differential—is often *perceived* by the employee as enhancing the manager's power while diminishing the employee's. This perceived power difference adds to the real differences that undeniably exist— the power to hire, to fire, to lay off, to recall, and to enforce rules of safety and acceptable social behavior. It is this perceived excess that we are talking about redistributing. And it is often the observable behavior of the manager, not merely the status difference, that magnifies the power difference in the mind of the employee.

Many companies like Jewel have recognized the importance of this redistribution need and are conducting similar efforts. While there is no assurance that "turning the organization's structure upside down" will dispel the kind of suspicion and negativism expressed in the first statement above, the chances of success over a period of time appear to be quite good. An extended demonstration by managers that they intend to follow such a policy cannot fail to decrease mistrust of their motives. Likewise, for the large majority of employees (those motivated to respond) it must foster independent action, initiative, creativity, and growth toward psychological adulthood.

APPLYING POWER REDISTRIBUTION TO OBJECTIVE SETTING

The joint objective-setting process is not a radical departure from what we might consider "normal" management practice. It differs primarily in the initiative given to the employee, in how the discussion session is conducted, and in the commitment of the manager to support the employee's efforts. It does not leave it to the employee to decide whether or not to participate in the process, nor does it release him or her from the measurement, review, and recycle activities that are the natural follow-up elements of MBO. Thus it does not deprive the manager of the responsibility or authority to require and get organizational change, but it does redistribute some of the excessive power often reserved by managers and places it in the hands of the employee.

If MBO is being introduced for the first time, the process should begin by familiarizing the employee with the meaning, purpose, sources, and characteristics of objectives, and with the role of each individual in the organizational improvement process.[8] A date and time for the discussion between manager and employee should be scheduled far enough in advance to allow the employee time to make a thorough review of his or her job description, the KRAs of the organization and of the employee's component, and the hierarchy of objectives (the means-ends chain) pertinent to his or her position.

Based on this preliminary work, the employee can formulate objectives in preparation for the review and ultimate acceptance by the manager, as modified during the discussion. A series of suggested forms, developed to assist in the documentation and review of individual objectives and performance, appears in Unit 6 of Vol. III. The first of these forms appears here as Fig. 6. Its basic format can help you translate key job responsibilities or KRAs into levels of excellence or other types of objectives. This work planning guide can also help you sketch in the backup plan of action necessary for implementation of the objective. Some organizations have found this format useful primarily during the training phase or early implementation of MBO, and have chosen to eliminate it when the overall process becomes familiar. Feel free to adapt it to your specific needs.

THE JOINT DISCUSSION

The employee's initial proposals serve as the starting point of the discussion. Sometimes called the *negotiating* session, this meeting must be characterized by free and open give and take by both parties to be truly productive. It is neither a formality, with the manager simply rubber-stamping the employee proposals in the name of power equalization, nor a sham in which the manager presents

---

[8]This is often done in group training sessions rather than individually. This series of volumes is adaptable to either format. If you are in a position of leadership requiring that you introduce MBO to a large number of employees, you will find the accompanying *Leader's Manual* useful in structuring your training sessions.

counterproposals (perhaps also prepared in advance) that become the final product without argument. If the session is to avoid these extremes, the individuals must be willing to "move." Hence the term "negotiation," although many managers rebel at the very mention of the word, probably because of its use in collective bargaining where it connotes duress and the threat of lost management prerogatives. We prefer the term "joint discussion."

Even though the purpose of this discussion is free interchange between equals, the responsibility falls on the manager to *elicit* free and open responses from the employee. To a certain inevitable extent then, the leadership remains with the superior and he or she must apply interviewing techniques that are unavoidably manipulative. We have no hesitancy in recommending these techniques, however. Since we have asked you to consider everything we say from the standpoint of both manager and employee, we trust that your two alter egos will get together and decide that manipulation in which the rules are known fully to both parties, and which is carried out in the best interests of both, cannot be all bad.

The rules of productive interviewing are covered in more detail in Unit 7 of Vol. III. As they apply to the objective-setting discussion, they can be summarized as follows:

1. *Listen, don't dominate.* The other's personality, thoughts, feelings, underlying motives, potential, and credibility can only be assessed when the interviewer is listening or observing, or both. "Shut up and listen, and don't interrupt," as communication authority Daniel Whiteside succintly puts it. An aggressive approach will quickly extinguish the employee's willing and active participation. A questioning approach is much more productive throughout, if it is used sensitively.

2. *Clarify facts and feelings.* The employee must have every opportunity to express uncertainties, doubts, and fears about the achievability of the objectives, and especially any questions about their relationship to his or her normal ongoing responsibilities. This is an important part of the validation process (which we discuss further in the next unit) whereby the manager elicits all information possible to assist in judging the acceptability of the employee's proposals. Any questioning done to obtain this type of information should be clearly understood by the employee to be in the interest of his or her welfare and success.

3. *Probe sensitively.* The manager must be assured that the employee's proposal is technically sound. It is entirely appropriate for these issues to be broached through searching questions by the manager, in spite

FIGURE 6

Work planning guide

Job Holder:

Job Title:

Major Responsibility (See note 1)	Levels of Excellence (See note 2)	Objectives (See note 3)	Plan of Action (See note 4)

NOTES FOR FIGURE 6

Note 1 Major responsibility

Starts with a *verb form* describing the activity (e.g., "To produce . . .," "To process . . .," "To formulate . . .," etc.).

Has an *object* of the action (e.g., "applications," "checks," "meals," "supervisors," etc.).

Contains *qualifiers* describing *why, when, in what manner,* etc. (e.g., "in order to maintain . . .," "at 3-month intervals," "to conform to . . . standards," "through use of hired contractors," etc.).

Use 20/80 (Pareto) rule in deciding whether or not to list.

Note 2 Levels (standards) of excellence*

Should answer the question, "Under what conditions can it be said that this responsibility is being carried out satisfactorily (excellently) (unsatisfactorily)?"

May not always be achievable within next review period.

Are best (but not necessarily) expressed *numerically,* with *limits* (e.g., "maximum of 0.1% rejects," "maximum cost of $0.80 per meal," etc.).

May need to be stated in terms of timeliness (with dates), *quality* (with definition), or *quantity* (as a time rate) (e.g., "all monthly cost reports submitted within 5 days after closing," "quality of service so that client complaints do not exceed five per month," "50,000 documents processed per shift," etc.).

Must not merely indicate present level of performance, unless specific action is neeeded to maintain that level.

Note 3 Objectives

Are stated as a *target,* or desired *status.*

Are quantitative, when possible to express in numbers.

Should involve *reach, stretch,* or *progress* toward or beyond levels of excellence.

Should be *realistically achievable* (i.e., backed up with action plan).

Must be *output-* (or *results-*) oriented, not activity-oriented (but see text of Unit 6).

Represent a *joint commitment* between manager and subordinate.

Are limited in number, covering *major responsibilities* (but there may be more than one for a single major responsibility).

Must contain time limits (e.g., "by November 19__").

Should meet all other requirements of sound objectives as listed in Unit 3.

May refer to Levels of Excellence (e.g., "attain 0.1% reject level by . . .," "decrease meal cost from $0.86 to $0.82 in first half 19__," "get halfway from current level to indicated level of excellence by end of second quarter 19__," etc.).

Should each carry a priority ranking with respect to all other objectives of the individual preparing the form.

Note 4 Plan of action

Who will do *what, when,* and *with whose help.*

If complex action is required, refer to Action Plan, Fig. 10.

*Not applicable when objectives are expressed as completions of project activities. (See Units 4 and 5.)

of our advice to listen not dominate. The competent technical person will regard such questioning as an opportunity to display his or her competence. When sensitively asked without an air of skepticism or distrust, the boss's questions are, in fact, a recognition of and deference to the employee's strengths.

4. *Maintain an attitude of helpfulness.* This is the last and probably the most important principle. If the manager can keep this one in mind throughout the discussion, the other principles will follow naturally. Every probe, every effort to clarify, every period of patient silence, every question by the manager should have the purpose of helping the employee express feelings, refine an idea, explain a point of view, air a problem, or validate his or her own objective. The commitment by the manager of whatever effort is needed to facilitate the employee's attainment of his or her objectives is the clearest and most substantial evidence of helpfulness.

The outcome of this discussion is a mutual commitment, a contract between the employee and the manager requiring that both parties collaborate to achieve each objective. The manager's agreement is often merely to keep hands off and let the employee finish the job in the best way possible (which may not be the boss's way). In many cases, however, the manager's help is needed to clear away procedural obstacles from the employee's path, to obtain added resources or funding, or to solicit the cooperation of other organizational components. These tasks should be accepted by the manager with a degree of commitment equal to that required of the employee. As we noted in Unit 7, the employee's need for support is an important source of managerial objectives. The manager's willing acceptance of this fact is the best evidence for the employee that the manager's power is being used in a benevolent and egalitarian manner. The whole MBO process will proceed more smoothly after this realization.

At the close of the discussion, the employee's objectives as originally proposed (or with agreed-on modifications) should be put into writing. A simple form can be prepared at this point (for future completion in the performance review process as described in Vol. III) as shown in Fig. 7. Like Fig. 6, this is a suggestion only, and we encourage you to adapt it to meet your own needs.

The manager's supporting objectives should be formalized in the same way and at the same time. There is no better way to implement and demonstrate the reality of the helping relationship than for the manager to accept this formal facilitating responsibility. (Such objectives should in turn be subject to review by the next higher level of management, just like any of the manager's other objectives.) The power redistribution process, which began with releasing the responsibility for selecting the improvement objectives, is made truly credible with this commitment of a significant share of the manager's own resources in support of the employee.

In popular terminology, the traditional "win-lose" confrontation[9] has been transformed into a "win-win" situation in which both parties gain from the transaction. Another currently popular way to look at this transformation employs the jargon of transactional analysis, which characterizes the traditional boss-subordinate relationship as a series of "parent-child" transactions. (Recall the widespread allegation that organizations tend to stunt the psychological growth of the employee, and our own contention that the boss-subordinate relationship is the most likely — though by no means the only — cause.) Transactions which have placed the boss in the ego state of the stern, demanding, omniscient parent, and the employee in that of the willful, backward, or naughty child, are carried out instead at the rational adult level by both parties. This level allows mutual respect for the other's technical competency and dignity as a person. Defensiveness, rebelliousness, and alienation on the part of the employee are reduced substantially, and the degeneration of the discussion into a series of win-lose games is avoided.[10]

There is a potential danger in the indiscriminate use of the helping relationship. Instead of converting to an adult-adult interchange, it is possible for the boss merely to substitute a *protective* parent role for that of domineering parent. Excessive help creates dependency in the marginal employee, while the achiever will feel smothered by the manager's attention and will resent what he or she regards as

---

[9]The term derives from game theory. The rewards accruing to the "players" (e.g., the parties in an authoritarian boss-subordinate relationship) are regarded as a constant, like the contents of a bag of marbles. In a "win-lose" situation, the winnings of one must be accompanied by an equal loss of the other in any confrontation or other interaction involving exchange.

[10]If you want to read further about transactional analysis, win-lose, and other aspects of productive interpersonal relations, you will find brief introductions in the "Lecturettes" section of *The 1973 Annual Handbook for Group Facilitators* (La Jolla, Calif.: University Associates, 1973).

FIGURE 7
Progress review:
work objectives

| Job Holder: | Reporting Period |
| **Job Title:** | From_____ To_____ |

Objectives (See note 1)	Results (See note 2)

NOTES FOR FIGURE 7

Note 1

Restate objective from "Objective" column of Work Planning Guide (Fig. 6) if used, or record directly from results of progress review discussion.

If entire objective is not to be achieved within the reporting period, add events from action plan that were to be achieved during the current period.

Note 2

Results may be in terms of quantitative or qualitative output, timely and purposeful activity, or critical incidents.

Note any reason for major deviation from plan. Corrective action should appear as a new objective.

Consider modification of objectives if changed circumstances so warrant.

Note any needed changes in information reporting system, added resource or support requirements, or release of resources unnecessary to assure objective accomplishment. Commitment to added support or resources should also appear in *reviewer's* objectives for next review period.

Work out any additions, deletions, or revisions for next reporting period objective statement. Set a date for submittal and review of next objective statement, if not done during progress review session.

unwarranted interference. The purposes of the whole joint objective-setting process are to allay suspicion, fear, and distrust; to create oneness of objectives; and to assure that the full resources of both persons are devoted to the job at hand. The optimum degree of help and power equalization is different for every employee, and only the manager can decide what is appropriate for his or her employees.

Nonetheless, the overall approach is applicable to a wide range of employee temperaments and abilities. For the *achiever,* little managerial input or help will be needed. The manager in this case clarifies the direction and overall objectives, then remains in the wings to help as needed. For the *developing but not yet completely secure employee,* a higher degree of understanding, help, and affirmation of potential is appropriate. For the *marginal performer,* more managerial input into the objective-setting process is required — shorter-range objectives with frequent measurement and feedback are advisable. The amount and nature of the help required in this case depends on the employee's problem. Help provided to correct a remediable defect is certainly appropriate, but help that merely enables the employee to avoid the hard responsibility for self-improvement is not.

The principles we have covered in this unit are best learned by practice. The exercise that follows provides an opportunity to do so in several simulated situations involving different types of employees and company situations. Two persons are required to carry out the exercise, one taking the role of the manager and the other being the employee. While the manager's role will teach how to conduct the discussion, the employee role can be equally valuable if the player will use his or her real-life job as the source of the proposed objectives. Further instructions on the role-taking method of self-instruction are given in the exercise (and more extensively in the *Leader's Manual* for this series, for those of you who plan to carry out group instruction in MBO).

EXERCISE 8 With a coworker (or with your boss or a subordinate), read the following situations. By agreement, or the flip of a coin, one of you will take the role of the manager in the situation of your choosing; the other the role of subordinate. Allow 5 to 10 minutes for each of you to prepare an agenda. You may wish to use either or both of the forms provided in Figs. 6 and 7 as you prepare for and conduct the discussion.

Carry out the discussion as dictated by the situation, applying the principles of power equalization that we have covered. Try to achieve a mutually satisfactory outcome.

Feel free to improvise reasonable proposals, questions, and answers. The tests of reasonableness are whether or not the proposals would make sense in real life. Questions are reasonable if in real life the other would normally be expected to have an answer; answers should bear up under reasonable questioning. *Keep the discussion forward-directed.* It is much more productive to figure a way out of a situation than to fabricate the reasons why you are in the situation in the first place—unless the situation statement gives the reasons and they appear pertinent in discussing future action. In negotiating the objectives, don't forget the characteristics of good objectives. You may want to review Unit 3 before proceeding.

When you have finished, switch roles and conduct the discussion over again, or move on to another situation taking your new roles. There is no time limit. Continue as long as the discussion is productive, then critique each other's contribution before switching roles.

If a third person is available, he or she may act as an observer and give you and your partner some additional insight into your performance. When three are involved in this way, it is a good idea to rotate through three situations, or repeats of the same situation, so that each may have a chance to take all three roles. As our commentary at the end of the exercise, we have included an observer's checklist to give you an idea of what to look for. You may refer to this now if you are taking the observer's role.

As you simulate this real-life situation, try to put *yourself* into the role. Rely *more* on your own feelings and reactions to the situation and to the other person, and *less* on the printed role. Try to avoid looking at the situation statement continually, or referring to it in such terms as "but it says here . . .", "Are we supposed to assume that . . . ?", "I don't understand what they mean by . . ." or in other detached ways.

You can introduce a great deal of realism into these discussions if the two of you can agree in advance on a role or situation of each general type with which you are both familiar, or which one of you can explain to the other(s). For example, in situation 1, you can take turns being yourself in the role of the employee. And in situation 4, you may use your own present feelings—as a manager or as an employee—as the basis for what a manager's objectives should be.

Situation 1 The employee in this situation is one of your top performers. You are a bit hesitant about engaging in joint objective setting because of the high level of his (or her) present performance and your uncertainty about how your demands for improvement will be received. Nevertheless, the company's targets demand the best effort from everyone, and it doesn't seem fair that anyone should be immune from these demands. You have very little to propose in the way of improvement in performance for this employee, but he or she undoubtedly has some things on the back burner, and your approach in the discussion will be to bring these up front. You plan to offer help where needed, but not to force your attentions on your employee.

Situation 2 Your employee is young, new in the job, and still struggling to gain a secure foothold. The demands of the job consist of much routine and often unplanned activity, and you detect the employee's tendency to get bogged down in this at the expense of needed project work. You sense that this employee has a great deal of potential and may be getting off on the wrong foot. You feel that one of a manager's greatest responsibilities is to bring out the best in people like this, and you are ready to commit some of your own time to helping achieve whatever objectives he or she proposes. You recognize, however, that natural enthusiasm and the desire to please may result in the formulation of some objectives that are not attainable. You must ensure that each objective is valid, without squelching the positive attitude and without giving the false impression that a measure of "stretch" isn't essential for employee growth.

Situation 3   This employee appears to be coasting. You inherited this individual with your position and have repeatedly tried to get improved performance in the past, without noticeable results. He or she gets the essential work done, but suggestions for improvement in the use of time or for assuming larger responsibilities go unheeded, or at least you see no results. You know that there are others who could and would do the job in a much more aggressive and broad manner, and you have resolved to give MBO a chance to aid in salvaging this marginal performer. You will ask for objectives and measurements, but if they are not forthcoming, you are prepared to present a few of your own choosing and to work out a firm schedule of reviews to assess progress. You plan to be patient and hear the employee out (you may find out what the underlying causes of the problem are), but also to be firm and not allow yourself to be used as a crutch.

Situation 4   Your employee is a manager. (If the person taking the role of the employee is not a manager in real life, assume that he or she is the manager of the component in which actually employed.) You recognize the temptation for managers merely to summarize the objectives of other subordinates and use them as their own. Some of this employee's proposals do not include the types of objectives you feel are appropriate for a manager, and you counterpropose by explaining how you went about establishing *your* managerial objectives and by encouraging the employee to do likewise.

Situation 5   As the general manager of your company, you are concerned because the staff functions in your organization have never really been subjected to the measurement that an MBO system encourages. Staff members are regarded by your operating units as the eyes and ears of the executive office, rather than as sources of new technology, advice, and assistance, which they are well qualified to be. You regard the reports that the staff provides about operating problems and status as valuable, but finally realize that your emphasis on this aspect of their work may be preventing them from expanding their responsibilities and fulfilling their potential in operations. You will propose changes in this situation, and will work with the staff employee during the discussion to formulate objectives and measurements that stress staff results.

Commentary on Exercise 8 This checklist of points you should have covered in the various situations may also be helpful as an observer's guide for use during the discussions.

A. General points to be considered in all situations

How much listening did the manager do?

Was the general tenor of the manager's approach one of helpfulness? Did he or she make a commitment to further help in achieving the objectives?

Did the manager use the probing technique effectively?

Did the manager succeed in clarifying and drawing out the employee's feelings?

Did the employee respond to the overall approach with new facts, ideas, or proposals? Did he or she appear to develop new understanding about the job? About MBO?

B. Situation-specific points

Situation 1:

Did the manager successfully avoid revealing the position stated in the situation that "everyone has got to do this"?

Did the manager show an appreciation for the higher-level needs driving such an employee?

How did the employee respond to the need for improvement? Did the manager contribute or suggest ideas for consideration?

How would you rate the conversation as a brainstorming session?

Situation 2:

Did either the manager or the employee suggest an analysis of the job in terms of routine, project, and unplanned activities?

What kinds of objectives resulted from the discussion? Better ways to handle the unplanned activities, crises, and emergencies?

Was the manager careful to avoid stampeding the employee into overcommitment?

Situation 3:

How well did the manager succeed in getting to the cause of the employee's problem? Was it boredom? The feeling that he or she has been put on the shelf? Lack of reward for improved performance?

Did the manager set objectives for solving this problem jointly with the employee?

What part did the manager play in setting the employee's work objectives? Was a future review date scheduled?

Situation 4:

In this situation you should look for employee development and self-development objectives, and those designed to remove obstacles hindering employee performance. Also pertinent are new procedures, reorganizations, resolution of pending decisions, presentation of plans, and other evidence of improvement in the *job of managing*.

The subordinate manager should not be allowed to set only objectives that are in effect his or her means for supporting higher-level ends. (Refer to Fig. 4)

Situation 5:

How well did the manager state the case for staff as technical consultants rather than as watchdogs for the executive office?

What kind of objectives were agreed upon? The transfer of new technology into production? The accessibility of staff members for advice and consultation? Changing the image of the staff in the eyes of line managers?

What was proposed to substitute for the watchdog role so that staff advice would still be available and most useful to the executive office?

UNIT 9

THE VALIDATION PROCESS

The validation of an objective — the assessment of the likelihood that the improvement target can and will be reached — begins with the preparation of the objective statement itself. The thought that goes into an objective to make it meet the many requirements covered in Unit 3 will by itself ensure that wild ideas are tamed and turned into more reasonable and achievable plans. The very fact that an objective is presented by the employee in the form of a written commitment gives pause to an individual who might have tended to make an off-hand promise with little substance to back it up.

One of the important functions of the joint objective-setting discussion is (as noted in Unit 8) the manager's assurance that an objective is technically feasible and within the capability of the employee to achieve it. If not, the manager is responsible for modifying the objective, or for committing his own or other resources to the task of improving the probability of success. Thus, we really began to get into the nuts and bolts of validation in the preceding unit. Furthermore, we will continue our concern about validity in the next and final unit of this volume, when we cover action planning, an equally vital step in the validation of an individual objective.

VALIDATING THE ENTIRE MBO PROGRAM

Skill in selecting and writing appropriate objectives, and commitment to improvement are prerequisites for the manager and the organization undertaking MBO, but do not by themselves ensure success. In fact, the highest levels of commitment and skill can work *against* the success of the program. Overcommitment can result in the generation of more objectives than the organization can absorb. A preoccupation with the niceties and fine points of writing individual objectives can lead to the neglect of fitting them all together into a workable package. Even when each individual objective and its supporting plan are virtually flawless, the overall MBO program can result in a net loss if it overreaches the capabilities of the organization.

Overcommitment can cause resources to be spread so thin that they are diverted from ongoing projects and routine activities that are essential to continued success. Of course, common sense will usually prevail in the end to put the organization back on an even keel, but even a temporary upset can be disruptive to morale and to short-term productivity. And if MBO is seen as the cause of the disruption, the firm is not likely to give it a second chance.

We noted the monitoring problems associated with proliferation of objectives in our discussion of pitfalls in Unit 6. We also suggested the bite-by-bite approach to objective setting as a way of improving the probability of successful achievement. In addition, we have stressed the importance of an action plan as an integral part of the objective itself. All these helpful hints have been directed primarily at the individual's efforts to set objectives that are useful, and at the manager who must cope with the added burdens of measurement entailed in the MBO system. Our emphasis has been on selectivity (recall Pareto's 20/80 rule) and on doing enough detailed thinking, planning, and negotiating to ensure confidence that the important improvement projects can be done.

PRIORITIES: THE PROBLEM OF RANKING ALTERNATIVES

We will concentrate in this unit on a two-step method for validating the overall results of the objective-setting process with either the package of objectives proposed by an individual or the collective proposals for an organizational component. The first step is a *ranking process,* and the second a *resource-allocation procedure* to determine the point at which resources are fully committed.

There is only one known cure for the profileration of objectives that naturally results when enthusiastic and concerned people embrace the MBO concept and become committed to improvement. This cure is the ability to place each objective in its proper position on a hierarchy of value or importance, and to establish a cutoff point that represents full use of the available resources. If a worthwhile project falls below the cutoff, it can only be implemented with additonal funding, personnel, or facilities. Otherwise it must be delayed until it is possible to proceed without diluting effort on higher-priority activities.

There is, unfortunately, no universally applicable method for performing this ranking process rationally—that is, without using a liberal dose of subjective judgment. True, a series of projects, all involving an expenditure of funds over a period of time—and a concurrent or subsequent return of that investment as increased profit, reduced costs, or otherwise—can be objectively ranked using such techniques as the discounted rate of return, average return on investment, or payout period.[1] However, even in this situation, which lends itself to qualification better than most, the final determination of priority is often left to subjective judgment; for example, which ranks higher, a cost reduction or the increased profitability from a new product, given equal discounted rates? What about a large project versus a small one having similar purposes and rates of return? And where in the rankings does one place a project to upgrade the appearance of a plant or office, where there is *no* tangible return? The questions become much harder to answer when the

---

[1]A classic article describing graphically the advantages and disadvantages of these various methods is John G. McLean's "How to Evaluate New Capital Investments," *Harvard Business Review,* vol. 36, no. 6, pp. 68–75, November–December 1958. A more recent article by Stanley B. Henrici, "Eyeing the ROI," *Harvard Business Review,* vol. 46, no. 3, pp. 88–97, May–June 1968, reemphasizes the continuing need for judgment.

costs and benefits are expressible only in nondollar terms — improvement or deterioration in morale, public image, internal communication, or other intangibles.

**SEMIQUAN-
TITATIVE
METHODS**
There probably never will be a fully satisfactory answer to questions like those we asked in the preceding section. You will need to rely on a subjective approach. There are, however, some techniques for assisting the judgmental ranking process. One of these is the paired-comparison method of stating individual or group-consensual preferences for one alternative among many. In this procedure, each member of a group of n items is compared separately with each of the remaining items until all the possible comparisons are made, $\frac{n(n-1)}{2}$ in all. No ties are allowed. After all these forced-choice comparisons are made, each item is awarded a number of points equal to the number of times the item was chosen over the others with which it was compared. Finally, the items are ranked in decreasing order of points awarded. This method is especially useful in ranking items in sets for which n is greater than 10.[2] For smaller sets, the items can usually be ranked equally well by inspection, with the paired comparisons made only on those items where the group members disagree on the order, or when there are a number of items (usually those intermediate in rank) that appear too close to call.

Peter Pyhrr, in his book *Zero Base Budgeting* (see the bibliography), describes another single-criterion ranking in which each project or activity is rated on a scale of 1 to 6 by each member of a voting panel. An activity is given a rating of 6 by the voter if it is an essential

---

[2]Paired comparisons in small sets often result in apparent inconsistencies or "intransitivities," which make the results difficult to interpret. For example, in a set of three items — vanilla, chocolate, and strawberry — although unlikely, it is entirely possible and rational for the choices to be vanilla over chocolate, strawberry over vanilla, and chocolate over strawberry. This would result in a three-way tie for the top rank, while a more likely (and transitive) series of choices might be vanilla over chocolate, chocolate over strawberry, and vanilla over strawberry, in which case the rank order becomes vanilla (2 points), chocolate (1 point), and strawberry (no points). In large sets, a limited number of such inconsistencies will not affect the rankings unduly. If a large degree of such ambivalence does exist, it is often the result of interfunctional conflict or protectiveness in the organization. Obviously, this issue must be resolved before the ranking process can be carried out in a systematic manner.

service that cannot be eliminated, and a 1 if it is clearly regarded as nonessential and a poor use of funds. A rating of 3 means that the voter feels it should be one of the last activities considered at the current level of funding. Ratings lower than 3 indicate the feeling that the activity should be cut off. The position on the scale below 3 indicates the order in which activities would be added if funding were increased. When applied to budgeting, the panel would include members of the various functions of the enterprise whose funding is at stake. A consensus under these conditions might be very difficult to obtain, and the final decision would be made by a higher-level manager.

An alternative is to add the individual ratings to get a total point score for each activity, and to then rank the activities on the basis of their total scores. A wide diversity of special interests among the voters can lead to a narrow spread of scores, however, and a superior may still be needed to break ties. A multidimensional ranking procedure such as we describe below may help to discriminate among closely ranked activities.

If Pyhrr's technique is used to rank an individual's objectives, employee and manager may constitute the panel, or the ranking may be done by either one. In many cases, a single individual will have a small number of objectives that can be ranked simply by inspection. The techniques we are describing become truly useful when an organizational component has more opportunities for improvement than can be pursued with the total available resources. In this case, the manager can, for example, assure that a high-ranking objective proposed by systems analyst A, but beyond his or her capacity, is not being preempted by lower-ranking projects undertaken by systems analyst B. The objective might be shifted to B, and some lower-ranked project deferred. A componentwide ranking of objectives can thus facilitate decisions that will improve organizational as well as individual effectiveness.

MULTIPLE-CRITERION RANKING

Ranking techniques of the kind discussed above are also useful in selecting one solution from a series of proposed solutions to an organizational problem, or in choosing among alternative action plans in support of an objective. In all these cases, however, a multidimensional ranking procedure is often needed to provide greater discrimination between alternatives that may be quite close in desirability.

Pyhrr describes one such procedure, again in the context of budgeting and with a voting panel involved. Each member votes on three criteria for each activity, again on a scale of 1 to 6.

1. *The legal or operating requirements for the activity.* At the low end of the scale are those which can be deferred with little or no effect on operations or legal ramifications. Top rating is given to those required to meet minimum legal or operating requirements.

2. *Impact on profitability.* At the low end are projects which have no favorable impact, while the highest ratings are given to those which have a great long- or short-range impact in relation to their cost. (Note that a non-profit-producing project could receive a very high rating if failure to execute it might shut down the business.) Pyhrr recommends that an agreed-upon intermediate ranking be assigned to projects meeting some minimum value of return on investment. (This rating becomes, in effect, the cutoff point as described above.)

3. *Level of exposure or risk.* The scale here varies from little or no risk in delaying or eliminating to delay with a high level of risk in relation to cost. Included in this criterion are those risks not readily stated in financial terms, for example, effects on employee attitudes or investor confidence.

The three criteria may be given different weights or treated equally. The weighted points for the three criteria are added for each voter and the resulting scores summed over the entire panel. Ranking is on the basis of this total score.

Another multiple-criterion procedure for ranking, proposed by George Odiorne in his MBO training activities, involves four criteria: *cost, benefit* (or contribution toward the objective), *probability of success* (or technical feasibility), and *potential side effects.* This procedure rates each activity on all four criteria, using the ratings of "high," "medium," or "low" on the first three and "positive," "negative," or "none" on the fourth. The ideal profile is obvious. Note that this procedure rates cost and benefit separately, rather than considering the cost/benefit ratio as Pyhrr suggests. Collapsing cost and benefit into a single variable is likely to cause some useful inputs to be overlooked. We therefore prefer the Odiorne procedure, for this reason as well as for its emphasis on side effects that might not otherwise enter the evaluation.

Confining the ratings to high, medium, and low has the apparent disadvantage of not providing a numercially determined rank order. It therefore provides no discrimination between the objective proposals or plans which have the same profile of highs and lows. This may not be a real disadvantage. It is often the case that the numerical treatment merely gives the *impression* of a degree of precision that does not exist in fact. In any event, once the four criteria have been explored for a pair of objectives, and qualitative values assigned, one usually knows enough about the situation to select one objective by a simple paired comparison or by assigning a rating using Pyhrr's single-criterion approach. In addition, if either costs, benefits, or side effects for the alternatives can be compared in dollar terms, this quantitative input should be used to sharpen the ranking to the extent possible.

You should use caution here, however. When dealing with a mixture of quantitative and nonquantitative input, it is tempting to attach greater weight to the former than its true relative importance justifies. (This is also a temptation in selecting objectives when quantification is stressed to excess. Trivial objectives that can be expressed in terms of dollar savings have a way of slipping in ahead of more important improvements that are more difficult to measure.)

THE ALLOCATION OF RESOURCES

In determining the validity of your overall objective list, you must be as concerned with overcommitment and its associated problems as you are with assuring that the most important things get done within the limits of your total resources. After the ranking procedure is completed, you are still faced with the question of how far you can go with what you have—dollars, man-hours, equipment availability, borrowed resources, cooperation by other organizational components, and so forth.

A mechanism for accomplishing this allocation of available resources among projects or objectives is the validation worksheet shown in Fig. 8. Use of the worksheet for this purpose is limited to

Job Title:
Major Responsibility (from work planning guide, Fig. 6):

Proposed Objective Statement (from work planning guide)

Major Requirements of Action Plan (see Fig. 10)

Validation   **Priority Assigned**_____
Use of available resources (see note 2)   (see note 1)

Availability based on (check one)   Present level_____
                                           Preliminary budget_____
                                           Approved budget_____

Amount and Percent of Available Resources Used	Personnel (Man-Months)						Other (specify)
	Employee time		Manager's time		Loaned		
	MM	%	MM	%	MM	%	
On higher priorities							
On this objective							
Total used or loaned							
Remaining for lower priority uses							

Comments (see note 3):

FIGURE 8
Validation worksheet

NOTES FOR FIGURE 8

Note 1   Priorities (ranked in order of importance)

Required, legislated, or base-load (routine) activities normally will be in the top priority category.

In ranking other types, consider magnitude of impact, cost in relation to benefits, and probability of success.

Contributions to other departments' objectives are important. A low-priority task to the person completing the form may be extremely high for the organization as a whole (see note 2).

As an alternative to ranking large numbers of objectives numerically, "high," "medium," and "low" may be more useful categories of valuation. Allocate resources (see note 2) for a complete category before proceeding to the next lower one. If you cannot accommodate all the highs, use paired comparisons to determine which ones should be cut off.

Manager and employee must agree on priorities, thereby assuring management's inputs and broad perspective.

Note 2   Resource utilization

If you are the manager, be sure to include your own time and other commitments to the employee's objective.

"Other" resources may be machine time, new equipment, capital funds, hired consultants, etc.

If desirable, resources used in required, legislated, or base-load activity may be subtracted prior to the validation process, and only the *discretionary* resources used. This is pertinent when only objectives to be monitored are major project-type activities. (See the discussion in Unit 6 on selectivity in monitoring.)

Remember to deduct for personnel or other resources *committed to other managers* for the achievement of objectives not in your purview (see note 3).

Sound judgment may dictate that a portion of personnel time be reserved for unplanned or emergency requirements. The percentage reserved is based on history and is a function of the responsiveness (as opposed to initiation) requirement of the job.

When all available resources (base-load, discretionary, loaned, and reserved) have been assigned, the remaining objectives (below cutoff) should be reviewed for importance and desirability to ensure against misassignment of priorities or for justification of additional resources.

Indicate amount and source of borrowed resources under "Comments."

Note 3   Comments

Include rationale for *reserved* resources.

Document your agreements with other managers concerning borrowed or loaned personnel. (Collaborative projects and objectives should be *jointly* ranked in order of priority and validated with all managers contributing resources.)

Identify and specify other resources used, loaned, or borrowed.

those individual or organizational work programs in which a number of major complex projects are vying for attention. However, any employee, including those with a single major project, will find the worksheet useful in tallying up the amounts of various resources needed for its completion. This kind of information, used in conjunction with the action plan (Fig. 10 in Unit 10), will help confirm the reasonableness of completion dates and guard against omission of key activities — negotiation of an agreement for loan of key personnel, for example — from the plan itself.

To use the procedure in allocating among a series of objectives, one of these worksheets is prepared for each objective. The first step is to enter the objective statement and the summarized requirements of the supporting action plan. The sheets are then arranged in order of descending priority. Before entering the personnel and other resources required for the number one priority objective, you must first consider the amount of resources already committed to routine, legislated, or continuing activities (the built-in priorities described in Unit 6). These are the job elements so often overlooked by novices in objective setting, leading to failure and disillusionment with MBO. These continuing demands on your or your employee's time should be entered on the line labeled "On Higher Priorities." Here you may also include a buffer of unallocated time reserved for unanticipated changes or emergencies. Only when this portion of the available time has been "mortgaged" can you safely begin the allocation to your number one priority improvement objective. When you have done this, the totals of time and other resources used are transferred to the "Higher Priorities" line on the worksheet for your number two objective, and the process is repeated. When the remainder of any critical resource approaches zero after the allocation to the nth objective, you have reached the cutoff point. (It may still be possible to borrow resources to pursue lower-ranked objectives, even though your own time and effort are fully committed.)

When you have determined the cutoff point, you should review the remaining objectives to ensure that their priorities have been properly assigned, and that one or more of them should not be pursued in preference to others originally thought to be more important. This, of course, implies that you must continue to exercise judgment as objectively and carefully as possible, even after the ranking process has been completed.

A FINAL WORD FOR MANAGERS

It is the manager's final responsibility to validate his or her MBO program, and to ensure that all employees undertake the self-analysis needed to keep the validation job from completely swamping the manager. A crucial component of managerial judgment is knowing one's employees (their capabilities, their tendencies to overcommit themselves, hold back, or use their talents and time fully to best advantage).

Upon being exposed to participative objective-setting principles for the first time, managers often ask, "How do I know when one of my employees is snowing me?" The only answer is to know your employees. Of course, there is no way of knowing with 100 percent certainty the *first time* you set objectives with an employee.[3] But if the situation recurs a second or third time with the same employee, the manager is certainly not using experience to sharpen his or her judgment.

As we stated in Unit 1, MBO is neither a panacea nor a substitute for management judgment. Neither can it obviate the need for technical knowledge in the areas being managed, or for the experience that enables the manager to estimate the amount of time and effort required to get certain things done. This ability is crucial to the validation procedure we have just described and to the action planning process as well. We will devote the next unit to the subject of action plans and how to prepare them.

---

[3]Good interviewing techniques can help. See Vol. III, Unit 7.

EXERCISE 9   1.   Consider the following list of possible self-improvement projects you might undertake or request to further your career or otherwise influence your future. Rank them by the method of paired comparisons according to their value and pertinence at this point in your career:

A college-level course in your functional specialty

A lateral assignment to another function

A voluntary committee chairmanship in a community activity such as the United Fund

A year's sabbatical to do advanced study in your specialty

An overseas assignment with your firm

Sensitivity training

An arrangement with a career counseling and placement firm

An assignment as assistant to a top-level executive in your firm or agency

Enrollment in a top-quality university executive development program

An extended vacation

Development of a hobby or avocation that will make your retirement years more productive

Employment part-time with a local community college or university as an adjunct faculty member to teach in your field

A staff assignment in your specialty

Participation in a series of management seminars on human relations

A course in creative writing

A reading program in management or technical periodicals and books

A management position in charge of factory or office workers

A management position in which your subordinates are managers or supervisors

Training in computers and management science

Team-building or other group development activities with your associates

Financial or estate planning advice from an investment counselor

2. Refer to the list of self-improvement activities in number 1, which you ranked in order of importance by the paired comparison method. Rerank the ones that are pertinent to your self-development objectives over the next 1 to 3 years, using the Odiorne multiple-criterion method described in this unit.

Evaluation (High, Medium, Low)

Activity	Contribution	Feasibility	Cost	Side Effects (specify)

3. Assume that your available time consists of your discretionary time outside working hours. Using the allocation procedure described in this unit, find your cutoff point. How many of your highest self-development activities can you make a valid commitment to complete in the time frame you selected (1 to 3 years)? Use the validation worksheet if you feel it will help you.

Commentary on Exercise 9   We can provide little specific feedback on your results in this exercise. However, it should be interesting to compare your original ranking by the single-criterion (or, more accurately, criterion-free) paired comparison method with that produced by the four-criterion Odiorne procedure. What influence did side effects have on your original ranking? For example, did you recognize the family tensions and the encroachment on recreational time often associated with off-the-job development? Or did you mortgage the necessary time for those essential activities as higher priority time *before* you allocated time to personal development?

How far your off-the-job self-development program cut into your top priority objective list will depend, of course, on the amount of discretionary time you left after allowing for family life, community service, recreation, and other nonwork activity. Don't forget to re-examine the self-development objectives that fell below the cutoff. Their priorities may take on a new importance once you have been faced with the necessity of consigning them to limbo!

Finally, we hope this will be more than just an exercise for you. How about getting started on your self-improvement program today?

UNIT 10

PUTTING YOUR OBJECTIVES TO WORK

Throughout this book and Vol. I, we have been preparing you —
endlessly, you may feel — for *action*. We have dwelt long and
searchingly on the many "preliminaries" to MBO but so far we
haven't let you go out and *do* any managing by objectives. Well, take
heart. As Peter Drucker says, sooner or later everything degenerates
into work; and now that we know where we are going, we get back
to the workaday business of figuring out how to get the job done and
then doing it.

However, our series deliberately leaves a very conspicuous gap.
In Vol. II we leave you *ready* for action. In Vol. III, our purpose will be
to help you assess the *results* of that action. We can't tell you how to
do the job that you have trained for in your specialized field or industry. Furthermore, there has been so much written on project

planning, implementation, and control that we will not add to the information explosion in those areas. Our purpose for including this final unit is not to take you into action, but rather to introduce you to several techniques and methods that will make your action plans more effective and your objectives more valid. The first two of these techniques come under the general category of problem-solving models — procedures you can use to generate alternative action programs to back up your objectives. They are useful, respectively, in two recurring situations: (1) the need to solve an operating problem and restore the organization to normal, and (2) the need to implement a major organizational change or procedure requiring acceptance by others over whom you may have no direct authority.

In this final unit, we will also discuss briefly two techniques for mapping out the action program itself: (1) a calendar of events, for simple programs, and (2) a more sophisticated network approach, for programs having many interdependent action steps.

PROBLEM-SOLVING MODELS: PRELUDES TO ACTION

The following models are based on the premise that anyone who has an objective also has a problem. The problem is defined as a discrepancy between *the way things are* and *the way we would like them to be.* This is an equally good definition of an *improvement objective.* The models provide a systematic method for developing alternative courses of action. Thus they are useful tools in formulating action plans when you are faced with a do-or-die objective (see Unit 7) or if you wish to make sure that the plan you have in mind is the *best* one.

The models we will cover are really variations on a basic procedure whose origin is lost in history. This procedure has become second nature for most successful problem solvers in all fields of endeavor. In fact, the only reason for presenting it step by step is to remind you that every step is important. Under the pressures of the job, it is often tempting to bypass portions of the procedure, usually to the regret of the careless user. Compare it with your own approach as we go through the procedure. The chances are that many of the difficulties you may be having in problem solving or action planning are traceable to shortcuts or failure to follow the sequence. Figure 9 illustrates the variations in the basic procedure: first, the Kepner-Tregoe model, which applies to specific operating problems — usually technical ones — where the purpose is to restore the situation to normal; and second, the Force-Field model, which applies to changes in organizational structure, procedures, or innovations that require attitude change and acceptance in order to make them work.

Step by step, the basic procedure, with variations, is as follows:

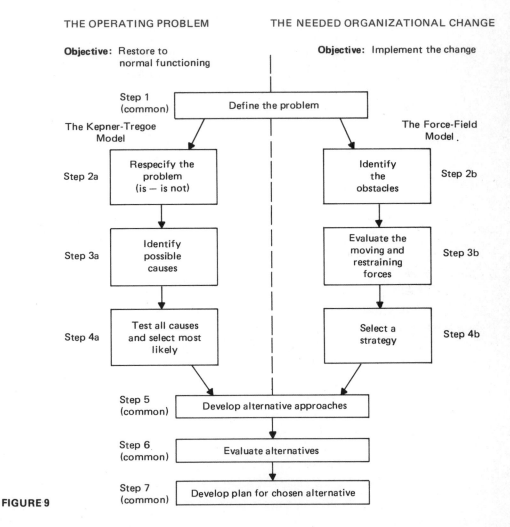

FIGURE 9

Step 1—Specify the Problem

Several problems may be involved in the "wretched mess" you are contemplating. Don't try to solve all the problems in your world with one all-out assault. The need to subdivide the mess into discrete and specific problem areas will become apparent as you proceed through the subsequent steps.

State the problem in terms of the discrepancy between the present and the desired states. If the two are difficult to quantify, express them in terms of behaviors or events. The desired state is your objective. Use all the guidelines for setting objectives appropriate to the situation.

The two general situations we mentioned above cover most eventualities: (1) the objective is to return to some previous state formerly enjoyed, i.e., something has gone wrong; and (2) the objective is to reach new levels of performance or organizational effectiveness not attained before—the true innovative objective. There are other situations that may concern you. For example, you may be faced with the need to forestall an impending disaster resulting from a forecasted change in the competitive environment. In this case, you need to take action to cope with a previously unknown situation, and it would fit the type (2) case. Most situations can be restated in terms of (1) or (2) above.

Since the procedures diverge to some extent, depending on whether the case is like (1) or (2), we will go through them separately until they reconverge in the later stages.

Steps Specific to the Problem-Solving Situation: The Kepner-Tregoe Model

Step 2a—respecify the problem Here we introduce the first variation, the Kepner-Tregoe, or K-T, process, for finding the most probable cause. (See the bibliography at the end of this volume for a literature source.) The K-T process begins with a respecification of the deviation or problem, which is examined from two points of view: What, where, when, and to what extent the problem *is,* and what, where, when, and to what extent the problem *is not.* This serves to isolate the problem, determine its true nature and magnitude, and prevent the manager from assigning causes that are too broad or are clearly irrelevant to the respecified problem. It further forces the user to identify *distinctions* or qualities which set the problem areas apart from the nonproblem areas.

Step 3a—identify all possible causes   A brainstorming approach is useful to assure inputs from everyone who has reason to suspect a source of the problem, or who has facts that may help to identify the source. Be sure to involve persons who have a thorough knowledge of the work flow and can identify all possible contributors to the problem. (These same people are also useful in step 2a to ensure that the problem is fully specified and all the distinctions identified.)

There may be persons who know the cause (perhaps their own error), or who may fear that it will be traced to their operations. In such cases, they may refute others' suggestions about the cause, if the suggestions seem threatening. This, in turn, can make the following step, screening the causes, more difficult.

Step 4a—screen the causes and select the most likely   The causes are screened by examining them in light of the distinctions— between what the problem is and what it is not—identified in step 2a. Next, the effects of each possible cause in contributing to the problem are deduced and compared with the actual effects noted. The most likely cause is that one whose *effects* can logically account for *all* the observed or actual effects—what the problem *is not* as well as what it *is.* If no single cause fits perfectly, the true cause may be as yet undiscovered (or "unvolunteered" as we noted above); or a combination of two or more causes may be at work.

There is another possible reason for failure of the K-T process to zero in on one sure cause when the problem has been recurrent or has persisted over a long period of time: one cause may have gradually or suddenly replaced another. In such cases, it is wise to reexamine closely the specification of the problem, and determine whether there has been a subtle change in the *is,* the *is not,* or in the distinctions associated with them, which would lead one to suspect multiple causation.

Having established the most likely cause, you are ready to examine alternative solutions to eliminate it. This may be a very simple matter, if, for example, the cause is a malfunctioning piece of equipment or a breach of operating procedure that has crept into the operation. On the other hand, the action needed to correct the situation may be complex. We will continue with the action-planning steps after we go back and survey the steps in the improvement or change planning procedure. We will then be at the same state of readiness to examine alternative solutions.

Steps Specific to the Improvement or Change Process: The Force-Field Model

Step 2b—identify the obstacles   Here we introduce a second variation, peculiarly suited to a situation in which the agreement and acceptance of the proposed change is crucial to its success. This is the *force-field* analogy,[1] which compares the components of an organization with particles of iron held in a magnetic field, caught in status quo until the balance of forces that hold them in place is somehow changed. The force-field model depicts the present position as the level of organizational effectiveness, competence, or performance that needs improvement. The forces are categorized as *driving forces* (whose presence prevents the level of performance from deteriorating) and the counteracting *restraining forces,* without which the driving forces would propel the organization to higher levels.

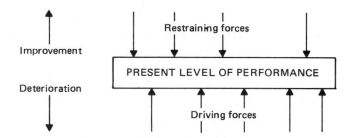

In this model, the solution to the problem of improving performance lies in decreasing the restraining forces, increasing the strength of driving forces, adding new driving forces, or any combination thereof. (Some combinations are likely to be more successful than others.)

The forces arise within individuals and in all aspects of the organization and its environment. They may be procedural, man-

---

[1]The term comes from the work of psychologist Kurt Lewin. See K. Lewin, *A Dynamic Theory of Personality* (New York: McGraw-Hill, 1935). This latter-day version is a simplification of his original theory, but it is nevertheless useful as an aid in thinking about resistance to change.

agerial, psychological, historical (custom, values, traditions), competitive, cultural, political (internal or external), economic, or technological.

This step of the planned improvement process consists of identifying all the restraining and driving forces that pertain to your situation. A thorough analysis may reveal potential allies in your change effort, and will certainly give you an appreciation for all the obstacles. Don't fail to consider key individual resisters and proponents (including yourself — your personal commitment may be the largest single driving force!). Also, identify the interpersonal or intergroup frictions which, while not actually restrainers, may act as powerful diversionary forces, robbing the driving forces of much of their effect. Finally, don't overlook communication as a major force, both restraining and driving. The very fact that the improvement objective or change has never been thought of, or is misunderstood, may be the major restraint.

Step 3b — evaluate the forces   A simple paired comparison ranking may assist your judgment in evaluating the relative importance of the restraining and driving forces. It is an interesting property of organizational systems that there is often a single major force of resistance that dominates all others in opposing a specific change.[2] This single force should be readily identifiable by anyone familiar with the workings of the organization, thus substantially reducing the task of ranking all the possible forces.

Next, you will need to decide which forces (1) are within your control to change, (2) will require help, and (3) are totally resistant to change or are outside any reasonable degree of control. If your single, overwhelming restraint falls under category (3), take time to reassess the overall validity of the objective you have set. Your effort may be much more efficiently spent on projects that ranked lower in your original thinking.

---

[2]Critics of "the system" might propose an axiom such as "Systems work most efficiently when the status quo is threatened," and therefore tend not to generate two restraining forces when one good one will suffice. For an amusing, but thought-provoking spoof of systems theory see John Gall, *Systemantics: How Systems Work and Especially How They Fail* (New York: The New York Times Book Co., 1977).

Step 4b—select a strategy   There are several basic strategies for effecting change. As we noted earlier, the first is to reduce or eliminate the major restraining forces, the second is to increase the driving forces, the third is to add new driving forces, and the others are various combinations of the first three.

Experience has proved that, when acceptance of change by individuals or groups is necessary for success, the preferred strategy is to attempt to reduce the sources of resistance (traditions, self-interest, fear, attitudes, beliefs, etc.). "Pushing" may succeed only in entrenching the forces of resistance.[3] There are, of course, exceptions to this rule. For example, when technological inability is the overwhelming restraint, the addition of a new driving force in the form of a technical breakthrough is the obvious choice of strategy. (However, see the discussion of side effects below and in Unit 9. Technical change has a way of breeding human resistance.) Another added or increased driving force that is often effective is a change in leadership. Properly applied, this new force can result not only in added *pressure* for change, but also in decreased *resistance.* Some resisters will decide to "go along," while others will enthusiastically embrace the new directions promised by the change in managers. Depending on your position relative to that of the leader in question, this strategy may be within or totally outside of your prerogatives. Don't overlook the great impact of leadership change, if it is within . your authority, and don't fail to review old projects for new potential when such a change takes place fortuitously.

One word of caution: if we err in any direction, it is most likely toward assuming that things are totally beyond our control, when actually they are not. While few of us have the authority of a chief executive officer, there are many things we can *affect,* even though we have no formal responsibility to *act.* Don't overlook the responsibility to:

> *Call attention to* an undesirable situation
>
> *Recommend* review or revision of policies or procedures
>
> *Monitor* a marginal situation to detect changes
>
> *Warn* higher-level managers of impending trouble

---

[3]See "The Role of the Defender" in *The Planning of Change* by Bennis et al., described in the Bibliography.

Many a significant change is initiated by those who have *no* responsibility or authority to carry it out. True, those who carry it out will usually receive the credit, but if you have the choice of dropping an objective as beyond control, or initiating some action on it before looking for new fields to conquer, we believe your choice is clear.

Step 5— Develop Alternative Plans

We have now reached the point in the two procedures at which we we can reconverge on the common final steps. These steps are applicable whether you are trying to regain the status you held before something went wrong, or to press for for a technological or organizational improvement. In the first case you selected the *most likely cause* (step 4a), and in the second, you determined the *major restraining and driving forces* and chose a strategy (steps 3b and 4b). The next step in either case is to develop alternative plans to eliminate causes, or to reduce, increase, or add forces.

The alternatives you develop will come from your own or your coworkers' experience and knowledge of the operation. We can offer only a few suggestions. The first is really a commandment: Don't be satisfied with the first plan offered. You owe yourself a harder look at the situation to ensure that something less obvious will not work out better. Besides, if your manager is a good one, he or she will *demand* to know the relative costs, merits, probabilities of success, and side effects of the other solutions you have discarded in favor of the one you recommend.

Second, try brainstorming. Alternatives can be brainstormed in private (simply list all the ways you can think of to solve the problem), but in most cases a collective effort can produce improvement in the number and quality of ideas generated. Organizational problems almost always respond best to a group effort, provided that the group selected represents all the competencies and viewpoints that bear on the problem.[4] Collective thinking lends itself even to technical problems in highly esoteric fields. To pick an example from current industrial technology, even the most skilled designer of microprocessor chips can benefit from bouncing ideas off ceramics

---

[4]See the *Leader's Manual* that accompanies this series for instructions on conducting a group brainstorming session.

experts, manufacturers, suppliers, and fellow scientists engaged in related work.

A recently reported technique designed to develop even more creative solutions is called "imaging" by its inventor, Warren H. Schmidt of Stanford University. This involves thinking of the problem as if it were already solved. First visualize the situation that would exist after the solution. Next, think of the conditions that must have prevailed immediately *before* the final solution was arrived at, and visualize the changes that might have caused that final increment of improvement. Working backward step by step in the same manner, you create a plausible scenario, or sequence of action, ending with the current status. Conventional brainstorming can be used at each step to develop alternative ways in which the step might have been taken. The rationale for this technique is that the first steps (determined last in the sequence) are not as likely to be bound by conventional thinking as is the case when the usual forward-looking sequence is followed.

Step 6— Evaluate the Alternatives

The output of the brainstorming process is characterized more by its quantity than its quality. Each alternative must be subjected to judicious thinking, and the total list pared down to the few that stand up in the light of informed scrutiny. When this has been done, the remaining alternatives are ranked by inspection or by any of the methods in Unit 9. We recommend the Odiorne ranking procedure because it forces the user to focus on the questions of side effects and unintended consequences that can negate any improvement that might otherwise result.

The most perceptive and meticulous planning cannot remove the threat of unforeseen consequences. But with proper attention to the evaluation of alternative plans, many of the unforeseens can be foreseen and their consequences predicted, if not avoided. Here again, the group approach is often more productive. Consequences of side effects can in turn be ranked according to their seriousness and probability of occurrence. Those of low seriousness and probability are easiest to handle. Those of high probability and disaster potential obviously must be accounted for in the planning—usually by selecting an alternative plan! The remaining combinations are troublesome. What to do about the disastrous side effect with a very low probability of occurrence is a judgment call. The tendency of most managers is to go ahead, focusing on the immediate favorable outcomes. (Most of us do, after all, choose the plane over the train.) Recognition of the possible consequences, however, at least opens the door to considering parallel protective action that will reduce the risk without paralyzing the project or the decision-making process. (Most persons who fly a lot carry extra life insurance, avoid single-engine aircraft, and take other precautions.)

Failure to carry out this analysis of side effects can carry penalties far outweighing the frustrating delay involved. We don't know the details of the decision process that resulted in the chemical "Tris" being selected as a fire-retardant for children's sleepwear. However, the revelation after millions of sets of sleepwear were manufactured, sold, and in use, that the additive itself might be a serious health hazard was a major catastrophe for many firms. This decision may have been the best that could have been made at the time, considering the great concern over flammability. There are other decisions on record, however, (happily of lesser consequence) that could have benefited from very minor additional analysis. For example, an organization concerned with the safety of children's toys

Disastrous side effects sometimes accompany the most worthy objectives and plans. (Drawing by William Hamilton; © 1977 The New Yorker Magazine, Inc.)

"I mean, you can have the cleanest air in the world but if you can't manufacture anything what the hell good is it?"

arranged to have manufactured and distributed to consumers a large number of buttons proclaiming the need to "think safety" when purchasing toys. Imagine the embarrassment in the organization when, several months later, the entire lot of buttons had to be recalled because of dangerously sharp edges and the use of paint with high lead content.

Step 7— Prepare a Plan for the Chosen Alternative

Planning for the more common contingencies is best handled as part of the detailed planning that follows the choice of the preferred alternative. The decision-making process we have described has tremendously enhanced the validity of the objective by its emphasis on correctly defining and specifying the problem, by identifying the favorable and unfavorable forces affecting progress, and by assuring that the most attractive alternative approach is selected.

THE ACTION PLAN AS A NETWORK OF ACTIVITIES

The detailed action plan is composed of subobjectives or milestone events and the activities that lead up to them. We define an *event* as the completion of a discrete activity forming a part of the plan. Events are usually stated as completions. Thus "prepare cost estimate" is an activity; "cost estimate complete" is a milestone event. The action plan provides the final evidence of validity—the degree of assurance that the objective can and will be achieved. It does this by answering the questions who, how, when, with what resources, and with whose help the job will be done.

Some objectives can be achieved by a simple sequence of activities; some of these can be carried out concurrently, some depend on the completion of others. If you can determine the overall sequence with confidence, you may use Fig. 10 as a record of what needs to be done, by when, and in what order. We have also provided space on this form for several reviews of progress to facilitate its use in monitoring as well as in planning.

In cases where there are many interdependencies among events and activities, more complex planning techniques may be necessary before you can provide reliable dates for the milestone events of Fig. 10, or even before you can be sure you have included all the necessary activities. Complexities arise, for example, when one event marks the completion of several independent activities, some of which must start later than others because they are in turn dependent on the completion of other activities. Other individual events may enable several activities to start simultaneously. These situations, and others even more complex, prevent the best use of Fig. 10 as a planning tool without first going through one of the techniques known collectively as network analysis. Included in this category are such variations as the program evaluation and review technique (PERT) and the critical path method (CPM). These methods graphically lay out a complex project as a network of related events and activities, as shown in Fig. 11. The initial event is the start of the project and the final event is the completion.

Figure 11 illustrates the complexities mentioned earlier. Activities 1, 2, and 3 (represented by lines) can start simultaneously. Event A requires completion of both activities 1 and 4 before activity 5 can start, and so forth. If the time requirements (in parentheses, measured in days) are reliably estimated for each activity, the earliest dates of all events can be predicted, including the completion of the project. The earliest possible completion date for the project is determined by tracing the longest sequence of activities. This sequence is called the *critical path.* Determine for yourself the earliest possible completion for the project in Fig. 11. (You will find the correct answer on page 189.)

There are many other valuable pieces of information that a project manager or controller can glean from working with the network. The earliest possible starting time and latest allowable completion time for each activity can be found. The probability of failing to make the required completion date can be estimated. Ways can be found to accelerate the project by rearranging sequences of events or reassigning manpower to activities on the critical path. These require a more thorough and quantitative study of network techniques than we can provide.

Our main reason for bringing up the subject is to illustrate that this more detailed analysis of project requirements can provide validity to your plans. This is sometimes impossible to achieve with a simple calendar of events as shown in Fig. 10. The quantitative aspects of network analysis, furthermore, are in our opinion only the icing on the cake. Its largest contribution lies in the identification of all the necessary events and activities and their sometimes complex interrelationships. You need to be no more of an expert in network

FIGURE 10
Detailed action plan

Objective:

Prepared by:

Date:

Milestone Event (note 1)	Completion Date	Man-Months		Other Resources	Review (note 2)	
		No.	Source		Date	Status and Action Required

NOTES FOR FIGURE 10

Note 1 Milestone events

Simple action plans involving few steps may be defined directly on the work planning guide, Fig. 6.

State events as the completion of essential steps in the actions required to achieve the objective.

Critical path or PERT techniques may be helpful in identifying all essential steps and the need for concurrent as well as sequential action.

Include man-months and other resources obtained from outside the department or component in order to define contributory responsibilities of others needed for achievement of the objective.

Contributory responsibilities or borrowed resources must be multilaterally agreed on by all managers involved. Unilateral inclusion of these is appropriate only in preliminary, tentative planning.

Note 2 Review

Two reviews are provided for each milestone event. The first should be sufficiently in advance of the planned completion date to allow for corrective or supplemental action, if needed. The second should follow the planned completion date.

Employee and manager should both maintain records of reviews.

Additional reviews may be entered on a blank sheet if required.

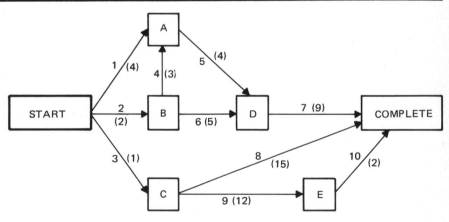

FIGURE 11
A simple project network

Activities are designated by number (1 through 10).

Events are designated by letter (A through E).

Arrows indicate sequence of events. For example, B must precede A, C must precede E, etc.

Time in days required for each activity is shown in parentheses.

The *critical path* is the *longest* sequence of activities between start and completion.

analysis than you are right now to extract that kind of benefit from the method. If you are curious, try the second exercise at the end of this unit.

As a managerial tool for validating objectives, a bit of elementary network thinking can be quite helpful. When an employee proposes an objective whose completion date or feasibility appears doubtful, think of it as a two-event, one-activity network. (The two events are the start and the completion; the single activity is the objective statement itself.) Work with the employee to subdivide the single activity into its components, and estimate the time requirements for each. This simple procedure will quickly detect any gross errors in the original date of completion, in the estimated manpower requirements, or in the match between the employee's capabilities and the skills required by the task. It may also be helpful to lay out the activities in network form to identify the dependency of certain activities on others, thereby further validating the completion date.

COPING WITH CONTIN-GENCIES

Our previous discussion of the unintended consequences of planned activities was confined to those external chains of events triggered by the carrying out of the plan. You must recognize the possibility of these events by brainstorming during the alternative-selection process, and then modify your approach to allow for them or to avoid them by using another approach. If the former course is chosen, the added activities (safety hazard analyses, reviews by disinterested experts, etc.) must be included in your planning network.

These consequences and the insurance you build into each plan will be specific to the situation. There are, however, several contingencies that consistently plague almost every project. Examples are cost inflation, work that does not proceed as fast as it should, supplier or contractor delays, the need to rewrite or resubmit supporting documents and calculations, and many others.

There are a number of ways in which the network and the constant monitoring of its activities can help in coping with common contingencies. For example:

1. In preparing the network, examine each activity in the light of your experience and assure yourself that the time estimate is realistic. Build

in an allowance for delays, or, if the final completion deadline *must* be met, allocate extra manpower or other resources to expedite or otherwise maintain schedule.

2. Cost inflation is a constant problem, which becomes more severe as the duration of the project increases. Examination of the network for all purchasing activities and for others involving major one-time expenditures can reveal opportunities either to delay or move forward these activities, depending on the inflationary climate. The time and resources allocated to these activities may also be increased to ensure that lowest prices and highest values are received.

   Cost contingency allowances are widely used in authorizing major project expenditures to avoid "coming back to the bank" for further approvals each time an overrun appears imminent. However, good project control dictates that an explanation be prepared for every use of the contingency fund, and that the manager review and approve the expenditure in advance.

3. Impending problems can be detected if actual versus scheduled progress is closely monitored against the plan, as shown on the network or the milestone schedule (Fig. 10), or both. Tracking progress on the network can be especially rewarding. For example, at some point an activity not on the critical path may be delayed or its estimate of duration be revised upward. Suddenly, the network may have a new critical path! Becoming aware of a situation like this as soon as it occurs provides the maximum opportunity to reallocate manpower or other resources to correct the situation.

You will find further examples of the potential of the network method in the literature. The limited treatment of the subject in this unit has served primarily to illustrate its value in validating your objectives. However, poor execution can negate all the effort put into the development of the most thoroughly validated objective. It is in the execution phase that the network method really comes into its own, and we close our discussion of the objective-setting phase of MBO with these illustrations of its usefulness, in the hope that you will pursue it further.

The earliest possible completion date for the project in Fig. 11 is 18 days after starting. The critical path consists of the activities numbered 2, 4, 5, and 7.

EXERCISE 10   1.   Consider a change or improvement objective that is important for you to pursue in your own organization. Define the driving and restraining forces that are acting to maintain the status quo:

Current Status

Restraining Forces

Driving Forces

2. You and your employee, who is manager of plant design and construction, met yesterday to discuss a major decision on how to expand plant capacity. The best alternative is to expand the present plant with an addition to the existing building, using present technology. Your employee proposes as his or her initial objective the approval of a request for capital appropriation within 60 days of yesterday's decision. The expansion is clearly a major project and must be approved by the board of directors. (If you are in a government or social service agency, use the obtaining of a major grant from HEW or one of the major foundations as your example.) Using your own company procedures, validate the employee's estimate of the time required.

(*Hint:* Your employee has, in effect, proposed a two-event, one-activity network as shown:

Insert the intermediate activities and events that your own procedures call for. Construct the network if you wish, but we are concerned mainly with identification of the specific steps that need to be taken to reach event B.)

3. We stated in Exercise 3, number 1, that it could be used as a post-test (a final exam) in objective writing. Go back to your initial objective statement (item a in that exercise) and rewrite it without referring to the list of criteria (item b) or your original rewrite (item c). Grade yourself on the improvement of this new version over the original, with respect to the criteria.

Commentary on Exercise 10

1. We can't comment on the forces that are specific to your organization. However, here are several, common to all organizations, that you may have overlooked:

Restraints

Restrictive, obsolete, or uncommunicated policies and procedures

The "not invented here" (NIH) factor

Rational resistance, by sincere, concerned individuals or groups, for very good reasons

Unawareness of the state-of-the-art technology

Top managers' values and preferences

Decreased responsibility for those affected

Increased responsibility for those affected

Poor past experiences with similar changes

Diminished quality, service, or performance image

Drivers

Your position in the organization

Pending legislation

Individuals or groups having like interests

Customers, clients, public officials, associates, etc., who will be affected favorably by the change

An organizational crisis

Economic necessity

Your credibility, track record, and other favorable experiences of others in dealing with you

Accumulated evidence supporting the need for change

A planning process that includes inputs from resisters as well as proponents

If you have really caught the spirit, you have already gone ahead and identified some action steps to affect this balance of forces, selected your approach (add to drivers, eliminate restraints, etc.), and drafted several alternative plans for evaluation. If not, we suggest that you do so.

2. Depending on your own procedures and problems, you might have concluded (1) "can do," (2) "it'll be close," or (3) "no way!" One company with very conservative views on allowing escalation factors, contin-

gency funds, and other evidence of loose estimating to creep into their appropriation requests, would require these activities (not listed in sequence):

a. Place on agenda of board meeting. Board meets once a month on third Monday. Agenda items must be submitted by fourth Monday of previous month. Twelve copies of each appropriation in its final form must be submitted at the *same time,* and must bear endorsement of corporate review committee (minimum 21 days).

b. Prepare verbal part of request (5 days).

c. Prepare financial justification (2 days).

d. Obtain three bids on all equipment (14 days).

e. Select engineer-constructor firm (1 day).

f. Obtain appropriation-grade ($\pm$ 15 percent) estimate of building construction and equipment installation costs (30 days).

g. Prepare (internally) layout of equipment for engineer-constructor (5 days).

h. Prepare building specifications in sufficient detail to allow appropriation-grade estimate by engineer-constructor (10 days).

i. Obtain concurrence of plant manager on proposed building layout and on selection of equipment (1 day).

j. Hold safety review with occupant managers (1 day).

k. Prepare complete cost estimate (2 days).

l. Schedule review of first draft with corporate appropriation review committee (corporate-level consultants on manufacturing, engineering, finance, marketing, and employee relations) (lead time minimum 12 days).

m. Hold review meeting.

n. Type and duplicate first draft of total appropriation request for review (3 days).

o. Select equipment for expanded plant (3 days).

p. Incorporate revisions and prepare final draft (2 days).

q. Type and duplicate final version for submittal to board (3 days).

With these rather stringent requirements for approval, you would have very likely concluded that "no way" could approval possibly be obtained in 60 days. (A minimum of 3 weeks is required just to get the project on the board's agenda!) The point is that it would have been impossible to tell whether 60 days was a valid and achievable target without breaking the one-activity network down into its component activities. You can also readily see the handicap that an uninformed manager can have in validating the technical objectives of a subordinate.

As an extra exercise, you may want to tackle the whole network for the seventeen activities presented above, and determine the minimum time required, if such problems are relevant to your position. A few hints follow.

You can get started immediately on preparing the verbal part of the appropriation request (activity b), selecting equipment (o), preparing the layout of equipment (g), preparing the building specifications (h), and selecting a construction firm to design and build the facility (e). Of course, you can't finish the appropriation request until you have the financial justification (c) to complement the verbal part, and you can't provide financial figures until you have the final cost estimate (k). This, in turn, requires bids on the equipment (d) and the contractor's estimate for design, construction, and installation (f). The plant manager's concurrence is crucial to acceptance by the corporate review committee and the board, and you don't want to start getting bids on equipment until the manager approves (i). The manager's approval is based on a safety review (j) with his or her subordinate managers, during which the equipment and the layout are closely examined for operability and safety. Note that it is OK to schedule the presentation to the corporate review committee without first typing (n) and distributing the final document (text plus financial justification), but that the finished package (p and q) must be delivered to the board at the time you request its inclusion as an agenda item (a).

You may also assume that decisions like the manager's safety review will go well and that your selection of equipment and contractor have been wise. Neither one will require redesign, cost cutting, or rewriting. (In an actual case it might be advisable to include rewriting or redesign activities in the network to allow for such slippages from the ideal schedule.) On the other hand, you should assume that the corporate review committee will have enough helpful comments to require the full time estimated for activities p and q. One final assumption: you are fortunate in your timing and find a place in the first available board meeting agenda, without having to wait an extra month for approval. (That is, you may use the 21-day estimate for activity a).

This is not as complex as it sounds. You can find help in resolving any problems you run into by consulting one of the references in the bibliography. But even if you do hit a few snags, you can, with what you already know, do a good enough job on the network to get an appreciation of its value in detailed planning and in validating a complex objective. The completed network is on page 196. Refer to it only after you have completed your own, of if you hit one of those snags.

FIGURE 12
Solution to
supplementary exercise

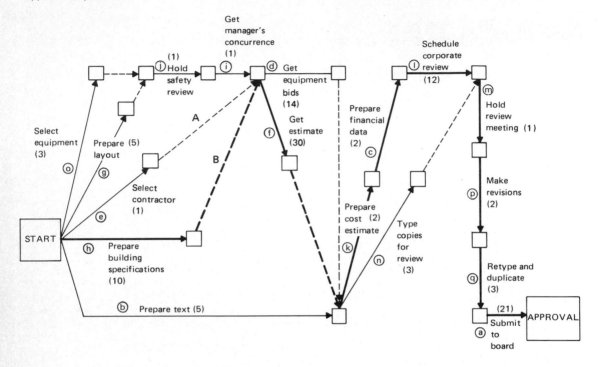

Note: The activities shown as dotted lines are "dummy" activities. They require no time to complete, but indicate that the events which initiate them must be completed before certain other activities can be started. (For example, activity f cannot start until both activities e and h are completed, *as well as* activity i — hence the presence of dummy activities A and B.)

The critical path is highlighted, and shows that a minimum of 83 days is required from start to approval. (The number of days required for each activity is shown in parentheses.)

BIBLIOGRAPHY

The literature devoted specifically to objective setting on the individual level is sparse. Therefore, we have included several works that should be helpful in familiarizing you with other terminologies and viewpoints. The chapters devoted to objective setting and validation in several existing texts are also recommended. Finally, because of its importance in the overall objective-setting and validation process, we have included several readings in the area of project management, planning, and control.

Bennis, Warren G., Kenneth D. Benne, and Robert Chin: *The Planning of Change* (New York: Holt, Rinehart & Winston, 2nd ed., 1969).

Written primarily for consultants, this treatise contains several sections of particular interest to anyone with an objective whose achievement involves changing peoples' attitudes. Chap. 7, on change strategies, throws more light on the force-field model. Chap. 9, on resistance, enumerates the many psychological and sociological reasons for resistance to change, and has an excellent subsection on the not-always negative role of the resister or defender of the status quo.

Carroll, Stephen J., and Henry L. Tosi, Jr.: *Management by Objectives: Applications and Research* (New York: Macmillan, 1973).

This book is based on research in industry done by the authors. Chap. 4, "Setting Goals in MBO," provides a look at procedures for objective setting from the top down, based on the research data. The means-ends chain is described and the importance of the action plan stressed.

Kepner, Charles H., and Benjamin B. Tregoe: *The Rational Manager: A Systematic Approach to Problem Solving and Decision Making* (New York: McGraw-Hill, 1965).

Explains in detail the Kepner-Tregoe problem-solving approach touched on briefly in the text, and proceeds from the identification of causes to the selection of alternatives that best meet the objective. A number of case histories are included, which illustrate the method and how it has been applied in practice.

Levin, Richard I., and Charles A. Kirkpatrick: *Planning and Control With PERT/CPM* (New York: McGraw-Hill, 1966).

For those interested in pursuing their use, this book provides a treatment of network methods in much greater detail than the Spirer reference (see below); it is still on a basic level, and very concise.

Mager, Robert F.: *Preparing Instructional Objectives* (Belmont, Calif.: Fearon Publishers, 1962).

Written for teachers and educational administrators, this paperback contains a wealth of examples (readily translatable into your own situation and terminology) of how to write clear objectives and improve unclear ones. Mager's emphasis on behavioral objectives, written in terms of desired changes in the students' demonstrated abilities, clarifies the distinction between activity-oriented and results-oriented objectives.

Mali, Paul: *Managing by Objectives: An Operating Guide to Faster and More Profitable Results* (New York: Wiley-Interscience, 1972).

Chaps. 3, 4, and 5 are devoted respectively to finding, setting, and validating objectives. The first treats the process of making forecasts of needed improvements. The second describes a number of approaches for assuring that all objectives are interlocked (see also Sherwin in this bibliography). The validation chapter contains brief descriptions of techniques such as decision-tree analysis, PERT, and the use of the work breakdown structure as validation tools.

Martin, Charles C.: *Project Management: How to Make It Work* (New York: AMACOM, 1976).

The techniques of project management are important to anyone setting and monitoring objectives that require many activities and the coordination of resources. This book contains useful advice for managers on improving the validity of action plans and establishing control mechanisms that save time and increase the probability of success. Nonquantitative in its emphasis, it stresses selection, organization, and management of the project team, as well as the more mechanistic aspects of project control.

Morrisey, George L.: *Management by Objectives and Results* (Reading, Mass.: Addison-Wesley, 1970).

A very concise summary of MBO, Morrisey's book has an excellent chapter (5) on setting objectives. Analytical procedures (production analysis and improvement analysis) are described for determining routine and project-type objectives. His treatment of the unmeasurables, which he calls "the *sub*jectives," is enlightening. He also lays down rigid rules for writing meaningful objectives.

Odiorne, George S.: *Effectiveness: Direct Action for Your Success* (Minneapolis: DirAction Press, 1967).

One of Odiorne's lesser known works, this book covers a number of personal effectiveness areas for the individual. Good in all respects, but especially pertinent to our subject in the sections devoted to personal goal setting and to the opportunities for improvement available through time management and work simplification. Good reading for your subordinates who may have trouble getting into objective setting.

Pyhrr, Peter A.: *Zero Base Budgeting: A Practical Management Tool for Evaluating Expenses* (New York: John Wiley & Sons, 1973).

How the budgeting process developed by Pyhrr at Texas Instruments, and adopted by then Governor Jimmy Carter in the Georgia executive branch, can be used to keep expenditures under control and channeled into the most productive uses. The techniques for ranking "decision packages" or activities (described in Chap. 5) are of particular interest to managers or individuals faced with the problem of deciding what objectives and plans should be cut off or retained.

Reddin, W.J.: *Effective Objectives* (Fredericton, NB, Canada: W.J. Reddin, 1975).

A programmed instruction manual, taking the reader through the steps of identifying "effectiveness areas," selecting and writing the objective, and completing the action plan. Of particular interest is the section on identification and/or development of effectiveness areas, which are KRAs as they apply to the individual job.

Sherwin, Douglas S.: "Management *of* Objectives," *Harvard Business Review,* vol. 54, no. 3, pp. 149-160, May–June 1976.

An interesting approach to interlocking the objectives of several organizational components in the support of overall company goals by the establishment of "objective teams." This provides an alternative method for involving staff components in objective setting: make the contributing staff person a member of the objective team.

Spirer, Herbert F.: *Project Management* (Stamford, Conn.: H.F. Spirer, 1976).

There are many treatises on network methods for project planning, but this brief fifty-page treatment will give a manager all he or she needs to know about the technology, as well as some good advice on how to validate the data that goes into the network (remember "garbage in, garbage out"?), and how to "keep your project from running you."

For greater detail on this subject, see the Levin and Kirkpatrick reference above.

INDEX

INDEX

Page numbers in *italic* indicate charts or graphs.

0-07-023191-5

Due